CARLO ANCELOTTI

CARLO ANCELOTTI

The Beautiful Games of an Ordinary Genius

Carlo Ancelotti
with *Alessandro Alciato*

foreword by
Paolo Maldini

New York · Paris · London · Milan

First published in the United States of America in 2010 by
Rizzoli International Publications, Inc.
300 Park Avenue South
New York, NY 10010
www.rizzoliusa.com

Originally published (except chapters 1 and 2) in Italy in 2009 by
RCS Libri S.p.A., Milano

2010 2011 2012 2013 / 10 9 8 7 6 5 4 3 2 1

Translated into English by Antony Shugaar for Paraculture, Inc.
Text design by Tina Henderson
Cover design by Gabriele Wilson

Printed and baund by
Nuovo Istituto Italiano d'Arti Grafiche, Bergamo - Italy
ISBN-13: 978-0-8478-3538-6
Library of Congress Catalog Control Number: 2010930884

Photography credits:
pp1–7, 10–13, and 14 (bottom) courtesy Carlo Ancelotti
p8 (top) © RCS Quotidiani
p8 (bottom) © Archivio Omega Fotocronache Milano
pp9, 14 (top), 15, and 16 © AP Images
pp17–24 © Getty Images Sport

*The author is donating all royalties from the sale of this book to the Fondazione
Stefano Borgonovo, dedicated to finding a cure for Lou Gehrig's disease.*

For *papá* Giuseppe and *mamma* Cecilia.
And for Stefano.

—C.A.

To Eleonora, who is my life.
And to JT.

—A.A.

CONTENTS

Contents

I'll keep addressing him by his first name; I always have. When a footballer stops playing, he can finally make friends with his coach. A certain closeness springs up, and barriers come down. I've been lucky in that I got that part of the job done ahead of time. I practically came into the world as a member of Carletto's team; we've always been de facto partners. People say that I was a banner for A. C. Milan. If that's true, then he was the wind that made me flutter. When the wind of Carletto blows, I'm out on the field, with my jersey, number 3, a perfect number in part thanks to my teammates. And he points the way. In his management of the locker room and team meetings, Carletto remains what he has always been: an unparalleled comedian. He manages to crack jokes even before the final game in the Champions League. He talks about roast dinners, he cocks an eyebrow, and we go on to win, because we are relaxed. People imagine that a coach has to make tear-jerking speeches to his team at the most decisive moments, and in fact there have been tears shed at times like that—but it was always because we were laughing so hard. On certain occasions, we've heard total silence from the locker room of the opposing team, while in ours Silvio Berlusconi and our coach were telling us jokes. We're a family, and that's what families do.

Carletto never goes overboard—with the possible exception of when he's eating, because once he sits down and grabs a knife and fork, you'd need an exorcist to stop him. Ever since he became a coach, he sits at a special table, with a special menu, and a special digestive system. He eats, he drinks, he eats some more, he drinks some more. When something good is served, forget about all his discipline and all his methods, including his beloved Christmas Tree. He can't stand to keep all that abundance to himself. So he starts calling us over: "Paolo, come here. You have to taste this." "But Carlo, I'm the captain, I'm supposed to set a good example." "And I'm your coach: have a little taste of this. It's good." He's generous in that part of his life as well. He enjoys life, and that helps us no end. Out of all the locker room management techniques I've witnessed, his is definitely the least problematic. He holds in all his own worries and pressures, and so the team preserves its tranquility. And goes on to win. And win some more. And keep on winning. From time to time, though, even the most patient man in the world blows his cool. The last time he actually exploded was in Lugano, after a pre-championship exhibition game against a Swiss team in Serie B. He looked like he'd lost his mind. He said the worst things to us, he peppered us with unforgivable insults. Horrible things, I couldn't repeat them here. He just kept it up, and I started to feel like laughing. He'd gone off the rails: I'd never seen him like that. He turned beet red, and sitting next to him was Adriano Galliani, wearing a bright yellow tie. Together they looked like a rainbow. Two days later, he came and asked us to forgive him, because he could never be mean through and through. He's a teddy bear, deep down. The secret of our track record is the fact that he's a regular guy. There's no need to be the Special One, Two, or Three to win. It's enough to have an inner equilibrium and to stay out of the limelight, to keep from setting off fireworks in front of the television cameras.

Carletto and I have always had a comfortable and close work-ing relationship. We've always talked about everything. Whenever he loses his temper, he unfailingly comes to me afterward and asks: "Paolo, was I wrong?"

Carlo never wants to do everything on his own. It's a sign of his considerable intelligence. And that's why he can win wherever he goes: at A. C. Milan, at Chelsea, at Real Madrid—anywhere. His knowledge of soccer is global, enormous. He has mind-boggling experience of every aspect of the game. Even as a player he was an outstanding organizer—of the game and of ideas. You can't really criticize him, either in technical or human terms: if you do, you're not being fair. At A. C. Milan, from the times of Arrigo Sacchi on, we've had lots of coaches, nearly all of them winners, but each of them managed the group in his own manner. Leaving aside the question of methods and results, if I were asked who brought the highest quality of life in those years, I'd absolutely have to say it was Carletto. Before he came to Milanello he was fairly rigid, less open to tactical innovation; but over time, he grew. He evolved. And we evolved with him, because you need to give a man like that players who know enough not to take advantage of him. Underlying everything that we did was a reciprocal trust. Over the years, there have been people who took advantage of the situation, but we were quick to make sure they understood how to behave. In particular, we explained to them that they had to respect Carletto, always, no matter what. Because of the magical soccer he seems to be able to conjure up. For the way he talks to his team. For the way he behaves off the field. And for the words he wrote in this book, where he has told the story of his life, and of himself, without keeping any secrets.

People have described him in a thousand different ways. For me, quite simply, he is a friend. A big, easygoing friend. And I miss him.

Paolo Maldini

CARLO ANCELOTTI

The Story of the Steak
that Couldn't Sing

Only once in my life have I felt like I needed a psychiatrist. I was looking at Yuri Zhirkov, but all I could see was a rib-eye steak. Perfectly grilled, juicy, smoking, medium rare. I looked him in the eye and suddenly I was starving. Which is nothing new, really. Meat, fish, red wine, Coca Cola, salami, mortadella, romano cheese, a chunk of gorgonzola, fish and chips, layer cake, an after dinner drink, spaghetti, bowties, pesto, Bolognese sauce, a rack of ribs, veal stew, antipasto, appetizers, entrées, dessert, and even—this one time, in a shrine to nouvelle cuisine in northern Italy—I had an espresso made from coffee beans grown on a compost heap, grown in the farmer's own manure, for all I know. In other words: I've gobbled down everything imaginable in my life, but never had my hunger stirred up by a football player. All the same, just then, that's what was on my mind: I had developed a strange new appetite. It may have had something to do with the fork that was flying straight at his face, following a trajectory that, I must say, had a certain elegance. Thrown by an unknown hand, with a clear objective. Ballistically speaking it was perfect, hurtling silently through the air, a clearly identified flying object. There was no plate, and the knife and spoon were missing, but the restaurant was there, and so were the diners: us, Chelsea Football Club. There was me, a manager with a slight trend toward waistline expansion. There were the players, hungry for victory. And there was him, a Russian midfielder with a host of talents and just one shortcoming: he can't sing. He just makes a lot of noise.

But now he was going to have to sing. It was his moment. If you want to join the team, it's not enough just to sign a contract. There's another hurdle, and it's the toughest, where pity isn't a word, where mercy isn't known. A player has to make it through karaoke night, a sacred ritual, and in this case it was being staged in a hotel in Los Angeles during our 2009 summer tour in the United States. This was my first time on the road since leaving A. C. Milan. Hollywood was just a stone's throw away and Yuri was on stage—I was trying to figure out if I was watching a slapstick comedy or a horror flick. More scary movie than comedy, judging by the shivers running up my spine. For players coming up from the youth team, the requirement is to dance in front of their new teammates, in front of the whole squad, a full audience. Players or new staff members that have come from another club are simply expected to choose a song and belt it out. Without musical accompaniment, without help of any kind: a solitary torture.

I, for example, immediately seized on a northern Italian folk song, in dialect, one that I've always liked: *La Società dei Magnaccioni*, by Lando Fiorini. The kind of stuff you'd hear at a small town party, where everyone's drunk. For those of my readers who don't know the song, I would suggest listening to Elton John and then trying to imagine the exact opposite. I did pretty well, none of the players booed or hissed. Maybe that was because they knew I was capable of benching them for the entire season ... No, really, they all cheered when I was done, and in fact somebody pulled off the tablecloth and began waving it back and forth, like a banner. They all surrendered to my bravura.

That's not how it went for Zhirkov, who had been introduced to the crowd by one of our team masseurs: "Ladies and gentlemen, silence please. It is my privilege to introduce to you tonight an artist who comes to us from the East, he's here tonight just for us, please lend an ear, and then you be the judges." The snickering in the background didn't bode well. From Russia, with fury ... The sacrificial victim was led toward the gallows, and by now I could see in John Terry's and Frank Lampard's eyes the terrible drama that loomed on the horizon. They were already laughing, even before he could open his mouth. Ivanovic was rooting for him— "Go on, Yuri!"—but it was the kind of encouragement you get when someone's setting you up for a pratfall. His teammates had been ribbing him for days, telling him he needed to train for this moment as if it was the Champions League final, that his future at Chelsea would depend on his performance that night. This was no joke, practically a sacred rite of passage. He looked as worked-up as I get when I'm about to walk through the door of a trattoria, and the fact that he's fundamentally shy anyway certainly didn't help. He stood on a stool and began. My. God. I've never heard anything that bad. It was a disaster, he didn't hit one note, not one. Pieces of bread were flying within seconds, followed by pieces of whole fruit—there was more good food on him than there was on the table before long. And that's when I started to like him. Eyes staring off into the middle distance, he went on singing like a drowning cat, like a stuck pig, for nearly two solid minutes. Garbled lyrics, a depressingly dreary melody: my old president from A. C. Milan, Silvio Berlusconi, would have summed it up with the words: "Of course, a typical Communist." Instead, the entire roster of Chelsea F. C. did something far worse: they let him finish the song. They refused to take pity on him, refused to interrupt that bloodcurdling cacophony, refused to let him go back to his chair in disgrace, go to bed without finishing his supper. And it was the last verse that truly screwed him, because when he reached the point where his teammates just couldn't take it anymore, someone finally let fly that blessed dinner fork.

I stared at it, suspended in midair. It was graceful in a way. It revolved as it flew, defying the law of gravity, like a precision missile. A very smart bomb, a bomb with an impeccable ear for music. As it reached the end of its trajectory, it slowed down and changed direction, like a football someone had kicked with a little downward-curving English on it. The fork was embarrassed, too. At that exact moment, I had my vision. When it comes to food and eating utensils, my brain is a one-way street, leading to my stomach. The association was instantaneous and organic: fork = steak. I smiled, and for an instant I was the happiest man in the room. Certainly happier than Yuri, who was by now tethered, a hostage, to his subhuman yodel. Čech wanted to put on his helmet to protect his ears. Malouda was the wildest, whistling and howling and stamping his feet as if he were possessed by the devil. It was a three-ring circus. I looked around for a red nose I could strap to my face, but I couldn't find one—no clowns, boys, not tonight. Zhirkov still hasn't fully recovered from the trauma. But thanks to people like him, and like me, like all the others, and like Bruno Demichelis (who is a genuine psychologist and a refined tenor, and who sang *Nessun Dorma* on that unforgettable evening), we became the team that went down in English soccer history by winning the Double, the Premier League and the FA Cup—not forgetting the Community Shield at the beginning of the season against Manchester United. For a long time, I thought that was my favorite trophy, if only because it's shaped like a plate. And on that plate you can put what you like: I piled it high with passion, with the discovery of a world I knew nothing about. London, England, Chelsea, Abramovich, Stamford Bridge, the Blues, the Queen. Another step in my life, another tile in this incredible mosaic, this splendid adventure. It began with that monstrosity sung by Yuri and it ended with *Volare*, that extraordinary poem set to music that I sang together with my team in front of the thousands of people who invaded Fulham Road, standing atop a double-decker bus, the day after we won the FA Cup final at Wembley against Portsmouth. A corner of the city had become our own immense universe. Untouchable, invulnerable.

It was all very nice, even if it was tough at the beginning. I didn't speak English well, and so the club sent me to take an intensive course in the Netherlands (in secret; and, at the same time, it sent all its top managers to study Italian—I don't know if that was a gesture of respect or because they knew I'd be a useless student). One of the reasons I fit into the locker room was thanks to the fundamental role played by Ray Wilkins, my number two and my friend, because it's one thing to translate words—plenty of people can do that—but translating feelings is the gift of only a select few. Ray is one of those select few, always present, noble in spirit, a real blue-blood, Chelsea flows in his veins. His heart beats in two languages, and that helped me. Without him, we couldn't have won a thing, and in particular we wouldn't have started the year at supersonic speed. The first game and the first trophy: the Community Shield against Manchester United, and we beat them in a penalty shoot-out: Ancelotti 1, Sir Alex 0. I had never been to Wembley before and it was a moving experience—maybe I was more curious than moved, but I still knew how it was going to end. We had trained too hard and too well to lose, I had absolutely no intention of embarrassing myself in front of my new players, and they had no intention of putting on a bad show in front of the new coach from Italy. I said to the team in the locker room: "We are a first-class group of players, but we don't understand that yet. We need to attack, impose our style of play, be recognized for what we do. I am going to learn a lot today." One thing, in any case, had already become clear to me in the preceding weeks: John Terry is the captain of all team captains, he was born with the captain's armband on his arm. Even without the band, it's as if he wears it anyway, and that's how it ought to be. He's different from all the others, Chelsea is his home, it always has been, ever since the youth squad. One word from him, and the locker room holds its breath. He's the first one to sit down at meals, the first one to stand up. Outside, he is the first, in the absolute sense of the term. Being part of this club is his mission, that's how he was made. He pays close attention to the performances of the youngest players in the youth team, he keeps up, he knows all the scores, he misses nothing (although he often loses at ping-pong in the dining room—and when that happens, watch out). He works twice as hard as everyone else, he has the sense of responsibility of someone who runs a company, a people, a philosophy that above all has to win. There is no room for second place; there can only be room for us.

For us—and in the end we went to take our prize. Climbing the stairs that lead from the pitch up to the stands was something I had only ever seen on television, I had always been curious to know what people think in that moment. I found out soon enough: "I have to lose weight." Jesus, yes, I have to lose some weight. I felt like I was climbing Everest, I was huffing and puffing, out of shape, I couldn't get enough air. But when I finally got to the top, I understood: it was like starting an ascent to heaven. To the sky. Which is the same color as our team shirts, and that can't be a coincidence. Once they put the trophy—or perhaps I should say, the plate—in my hand, I hoisted it with enormous pride. Priceless, unique, and incredibly light. Magic seconds. And then an imperceptible sense of discomfort seized hold of me for an instant; but that always happens when I see an empty plate.

CHAPTER 2

Times Tables and Victory

Soccer is like having lunch with your friends: the more you eat, the hungrier you get. It's the chef and the company that make all the difference; and I love the company of David Beckham. One evening, while he was playing for A. C. Milan, I invited Beckham to dinner in a restaurant in Parma. By the end of the evening, he refused to leave the restaurant. I kept insisting, and he kept pleading with me, "Please, one more course." At one point I considered calling the police—handcuffs would certainly have stopped him from cramming any more tortellini into his mouth. In the end, I managed to convince him with these words: "Look, David, if we don't leave this restaurant right now, I'm going to arrange another Spice Girls reunion tour." Fourteen seconds later we were back in the car, hurtling back toward Milan, with the radio off. Open parenthesis: Let me say something about David. He was a big surprise to me, and a positive one. When he arrived in Italy, I expected to be dealing with a movie star homesick for Los Angeles, one of those players who thinks too much about gossip and fame and not enough about football. But I was wrong. He's an impeccable professional, a workaholic, and an almost excessively well-mannered gentleman, with all the class of a very honest person. And then there's the fact that he likes Emilian delicacies, which is obviously what matters most. Close parenthesis.

We never had time to go back, but one day I'll return to Parma with my Chelsea players. And there's only one problem to overcome as far as they're concerned: the sun shines in Parma, so they'll be disoriented, especially Lampard and Terry, the English ones ... They'll look up at that strange orange ball in the middle of the sky, scratch their heads, and ask in unison: "Uh, what's that?" They'll be frightened, even more frightened than they were when they heard Zhirkov singing karaoke. They've never seen the sun in their lives. I have, but in my first ten days in London, I came close to forgetting what it looks like. It rained. The whole time. Day and night, around the clock. I left the house in the morning like a small child strolling down Ocean Drive on his way to the beach in Miami, without a bucket and spade but wearing a short-sleeved shirt, and I'd come home in the evening like an Alaskan sleigh dog, without a tail but chilled to the bone. All the same, I got used to the cold weather, and I got used to my new life: the English were a crucial part of that. I can go wherever I want without being stopped on the street, that's the exciting new change for me. I can go to the supermarket and the only people who come up to me are security guards, looking at my overflowing shopping cart and wondering, with a hint of suspicion, "Is this a robbery?" Other people recognize me but they treat me like one of them. They leave me alone, they respect my privacy, and nearly all the autographs I signed this year were for Italian fans, who nonetheless have a place in my heart and always will. It's an attitude that makes up a part of a larger picture, the culture of football fans in England: people go to the stadium to cheer on their team; you know that if you make a mistake you'll pay for it; there are kids in the stands, not guys with baseball bats. And a manager can live without as much pressure, there's more leisure time—time to think, time to live your life, and time to work better.

And, in my case, time to win. In the Premier League, we began in grand style, encouraged by Abramovich's request ("I want Chelsea's style of play to be recognized around the world") and by the formation that I brought with me from Italy: 4-3-2-1, the Christmas tree. The first few times, no one got it—not the sports journalists, not even the coaches of the opposing teams. For a while, it was a walk in the park, I was enjoying myself enormously, and the 3-1 that we stuck to Sunderland in the second game of the season felt almost like a physical pleasure. It was like running downhill: our confidence grew, and the players were happy, too, because they were trying something new—they weren't bored. I would change the way we played depending on Anelka's position. Things went great until December, when our opponents started to figure out how to beat us, and our winning streak started to flag, which was inevitable anyway. We lost to Manchester City, and we drew with Everton, West Ham, and Birmingham. It's normal not to win every match in a season; when people said we should never lose a game I wanted to laugh, but it made me laugh just as hard when they said we'd never bring the trophies home . . . We recovered and we started running again at our own pace, and without giving away too many secrets. For one simple reason: there aren't any secrets— or maybe just one.

A times table. Like the ones they give you in elementary school, when you learn to count and do multiplication. You slide beads on an abacus, you count sheep before falling asleep (to tell the truth, I always counted lambs, they're tender and easier to digest), and over time the arithmetic filters into your mind. We did our calculations right after we were catapulted out of the running for the Champions League by Inter, then Champions of Europe, at a moment in the season that was so precarious it could easily have slid into disaster. In the past, Chelsea had always had a hard time recovering from roundhouse punches like that, so the day after our defeat we all gathered in the locker room of our training grounds in Cobham. The venerable old men all spoke—Terry, Drogba, Cech, and Lampard (another magnificent example of English leadership; when I see him on the field, it makes me happy). I was proud of us in that twenty minutes, we understood that we had lost a great deal but that we could win much, much more. I was very clear in what I had to say: "The Premiership and the FA Cup are still ours for the taking. Only six teams have managed to pull off a double in 140 years, but boys, it's our turn now." The plan— and it wasn't exactly a secret plan—was to deflect attention from the Champions League and focus our energies on a new target. "We're eleven games from the end of the season, and if we play them well we can go down in history." At that point, we pulled out our times table. Numbers and statistics, written so clearly that no one could possibly misunderstand. There were only a few numbers, simple, fundamental sums that we needed to keep in mind. The number of training sessions remaining: 50. The number of days we could still devote to achieving our objectives: 60, more or less. The number of games left to play: 11.

The first game was against Blackburn, and to tell the truth, the final score of 1-1 did sort of scare me. Then we exploded like an atomic bomb: 5-0 against Portsmouth, 7-1 against Aston Villa, 2-1 away to Manchester United. All magic numbers that made our times table look pretty special. Our success at Old Trafford was the one that got us the League title, even though in the end Ray Wilkins and I were forced to drink to our victory alone. As is the tradition, a few minutes after the final whistle we went to Sir Alex's room to drink the usual glass of wine. We walked in, and silence reigned. He sat there staring at a television screen; the set was tuned to a horse race, his greatest love. We were strictly relegated to the background, to some place beyond and behind the background. We stood awkwardly for a while without saying a word, uncertain what to do, and finally did what we had come to do: we drank a glass of wine, to our own health. Bye-bye. Even though I won each of the three games I played against him that season, I still consider Ferguson to be a master of soccer, a teacher in my life, an example I have always looked up to, a colleague to emulate, and in fact, in some ways, unattainable. (Unattainable in the sense that I don't have a passion for racehorses.) Before heading back to Stamford Bridge, we took on Aston Villa in the FA Cup: 3-0.

Then in the League again: 1-0 at Bolton, we took a beating from Tottenham, we gave 7 to Stoke, then 2-0 against Liverpool, and 8-0 against Wigan. We became Champions of England, I was a foreign king in a friendly country. A slightly tipsy king, if you want to know the truth, because I've only seen as much beer in one place as there was in our locker room a few times. The boys were dancing to rap music; I gave it a try too, but without much luck— I have a hard time rhyming credibly in English. I wasn't thinking all that clearly, and that was when I decided to make a little speech to my team: "*Carissimi signori*, the time has come for you to start learning Italian. We're colonizing you now. I train Chelsea Champions, Capello is the manager of the National Team..." Obi Mikel, Joe Cole, and Drogba (who is a machine on the field), Malouda (the player who most impressed me with the way he improved) all gave me their approval, in their way: "Oh, you're right, Carlo, *e che cazzo* ..." I must have missed something, apparently. *Eccheccazzo sì*—Italian for "what the fuck"—they knew Italian better than I did. Couldn't they have told me before?

We each pulled out our times tables. We realized that there was still a problem left to solve, the result of the FA Cup final. From which I cherish one memory in particular: Prince William saying hello before the game, with the teams already lined up on the field at Wembley. I introduced the players to him, one by one, and after that he simply said, "Good luck." For a minute I wanted to reply with a question: "Will you introduce me to your grandmother?" But I didn't have the courage. I have an abiding veneration for Queen Elizabeth, I don't know her personally but whenever I see her on television I find her fascinating as a person. I'd like to meet her, though I don't know how I could arrange it. It's not like I can call Buckingham Palace and ask to be put through. "Hello, excuse me, this is Carlo Ancelotti—you know, the one who eats too much. Could I speak to Elizabeth, please?" It's just not done. So all I can do is keep winning, and hope that she notices. With her grandson watching, we won the Cup, beating Portsmouth 1-0 after hitting the goalposts five times in the first half.

There are days when it feels like I'm living a dream. I would make the same decision—to coach Chelsea—a hundred times, the same decision every time. Even if getting knocked out of the running for the Champions League against Inter is a regret that will always be with me. Against Inter, not against Mourinho. In Italy, we said plenty of harsh things to one another, we didn't particularly like each other (read this book, you'll understand . . .), but ever since I've been in England my point of view has changed. He made history at the club where I work, his archive of training sessions and exercises has been useful to me more than once, and so he deserves total and rapt attention. We decided to call a truce—a truce signed and agreed before the first leg of our match in the Champions League, in Milan. We met in a corridor at the San Siro, and we made a pact: "No more bickering, no more controversy." Six words, a handshake, and in ten seconds we had an understanding. People often ask me: why did you get knocked out of the Champions League against Inter? Answer: it was a matter of details. There aren't any other truths, there's nothing else to be said. I don't think José and I will ever be friends, but now we have a real and reciprocal respect. When I won the Premiership, he wrote me a text message: "Champagne." When he won the Scudetto in Italy, I sent him a text message back: "Champagne, but not too much."

No matter how you look at it, it always comes back to food and drink. Chelsea Football Club, with lots of bubbles. My new life. And the taxi cab where it all started.

CHAPTER 3

Summoned for a Meeting
with Abramovich. It Begins.

I have to say, this taxi driver is starting to make me uneasy. He's staring into the rearview mirror, but what he's really doing is monitoring my expression. He's looking for answers, answers I can't give him, at least not yet. I'm traveling incognito, rushing headlong into some kind of illicit affair, or at least that's the impression I'm giving. It feels odd—unlike me. The coach of the A. C. Milan team on an undercover mission. My heartbeat is normal; that's probably because my mind is busy. Working, thinking. And even, every so often, playing.

Here I am, 007 on a top-secret mission for myself. Sitting behind a driver with the face of an assassin. Perhaps it all makes sense, all things considered, because in a way it's my life that's at stake. My future. It's as if I'm riding in a time machine, not a taxi cab: from Milanello to Stamford Bridge, from yesterday to today, from one (red and black) devil to another, one I don't yet know. Oh, I forgot to mention, I'm in Paris, and this taxi is taking me to my appointment with Roman Abramovich, the self-made Russian billionaire and, more importantly—as far as I'm concerned—the deep-pocketed owner of Chelsea Football Club, who's looking for a new coach.

No one else knows, but we've already had one meeting, a couple of weeks ago. It was in Switzerland, in a grand hotel in Geneva, not far from the city center; I'd tell you its name, I really would, but I swear I can't remember it. I must be getting old. Charlie Stillitano organized the meeting; he's a friend of mine who works in the world of soccer in the United States. He knows Peter Kenyon, Abramovich's chief executive at Chelsea. As soon as the soccer season ended, apparently, Kenyon said he wanted a meeting with me. No sooner said than done. I was vacationing on the lake, sunning myself in the fresh water, soaking away the bitter taste of Milan's failure to qualify for the Champions League. Abramovich came to see me, which is a good sign, but . . . the guy certainly has a lot of bodyguards! They met me and ushered me in to see the Big Boss and Kenyon; the welcoming committee was rounded out by another executive, a lawyer, and an interpreter. We all sat down, got comfortable, and said our friendly hellos. Then we began to talk. About soccer: nothing but soccer, all soccer, all the time.

For sticklers about dates, it was May 2008. Abramovich wanted to know everything about me, about the way I work, about my philosophy. He was looking for a team with a clear identity. As he told me: "Like Manchester United, Liverpool, or Milan—

certainly not my Chelsea." As he talked, my curiosity grew. He was nothing like the monster described in the press. Quite the opposite. The first thing that struck me was how shy he seemed to be. The second thing was what an expert he was on soccer: he knew the game inside out. The third thing was his ravenous appetite for success: "My dear Ancelotti, I want to win. I want to win everything." In fact, he immediately reminded me of someone, another team owner, if you follow my drift... After all was said and done, I came away with an excellent impression of him. The hour flew by, an hour's conversation in which he never once mentioned money. "Goodbye, look forward to meeting you again soon."

And now here we are. The Hotel George V, a luxurious place just a short walk from the Champs-Elysées, with a magnificent terrace overlooking all of Paris and, for that matter, today at least, London. I thank the cabbie-torpedo-psychoanalyst as I get out of the car, I give him a generous tip—better safe than sorry—and I proceed toward my top-secret destination. Abramovich and me, Act II.

This has to remain a secret, no one can know about it. That's one thing everyone agrees on. I'm wearing sunglasses, I scan the street with the expression of a well-trained secret agent: check, it's all clear, no photographers loitering outside the hotel lobby. Just a few blocks from here, yesterday, they caught Massimo Moratti having lunch with José Mourinho—the chairman and the future coach of Inter. I can't let that happen to me. Nope, the coast is clear, no one looks suspicious, I can go in. What a magnificent lobby, what a luxurious atmosphere. What ... the fuck? No, it can't be. I can't believe my eyes. Clear across the lobby, in a secluded corner, is Federico Pastorello, an Italian soccer agent, and a close personal acquaintance. Do you know the sound of the buzzer when a contestant gets something wrong on a quiz show? Well, as I'm standing there in the lobby of the Hotel George V, that's the sound that's echoing in my ears. And beneath it, a tiny little voice that sounds a lot like my own, whispering: "asshole." No, listen closer. That's "Asshole." With a capital 'A.'

Now what do I do? I hide. Over there, on the far side of the lobby, there's a little sitting room, an alcove, that'll be perfect. If I move fast, I can just duck in. Whew! I'm safe. No, I'm not. I hear the buzzer, I hear that tiny familiar voice. Maybe I'm being featured on an episode of *Candid Camera*—there sits a close friend and colleague. Another Italian coach, in fact, who works in a city that is dear to my heart. I laugh. "So what are you doing here?"

"No, what are *you* doing here?"

I laugh again. This port in a storm, this chance refuge is starting to seem crowded. For a brief instant, I feel as if I'm at the supermarket. All of us here for a meeting with this chairman, but the merchandise on display is us. A waiting room for the two of us, or maybe for three, or a hundred, who knows how many of us there are. Awareness dawns, I feel a chill, but still, I'm here to meet with him. I step downstairs. He's waiting for me in a grand meeting room, designed for a much larger crowd. Sitting around the table are the same people who were there in Geneva.

I want to make one thing clear from the start. "I have a contract with A. C. Milan, I'm perfectly happy there. If I wind up working with Chelsea, it can only be if Milan is in agreement."

Again, the topic is all soccer, all the time. The inevitable question:

how would I change the way Chelsea plays, if we were to come to an understanding?

"Chairman, your team is very physical, they need to field a more diverse array of skills."

I come up with a couple of names, Franck Ribéry and Xabi Alonso, players that would give the team a distinct advantage. He comes up with a third name: Andriy Shevchenko, a player he clearly cares about deeply: "I can't figure out why he's not playing, ever since we brought him to England, he's just not the real Sheva anymore, I don't know why he's having so much trouble."

"Chairman, I can't possibly tell you the reason." So we talk, and we talk, and we talk some more. I'm very comfortable chatting with Abramovich. He's not intimidating, even when he says to me, with a slight catch in his voice: "Look, we just lost out on the Champions League finals, we just got bounced out of the championship, I have nothing to be happy about. Chelsea just seems to lack personality. My ambition is to win every game my team plays, but right now I just don't recognize my team." He cares very much about winning and about playing the game with style. Again, he reminds me of someone. There go another forty minutes, like a flash. "Thanks very much, Ancelotti, we'll be in touch." Not a word about money. OK, I can read between the lines. There's no opening just now.

I walk upstairs, I see daylight. In the true sense of the word. But I no longer see Pastorello, nor do I see my friend and colleague and fellow coach. They've all vanished. So I vanish, too. I go out for a walk, and Paris beckons. A couple of hours go by, my phone rings.

"Hello, this is Adriano Galliani: how's Paris?" Pause. The vice-president of A. C. Milan. "How's your little fling going?"

He already knows everything. Caught red-handed, like Moratti and Mourinho. It wasn't a fling, nothing happened, now it's clear to me, and I tell him so immediately: "I came to have a meeting with Abramovich. When the owner of such an important team calls you, the very least you can do is go and listen to what he has to say."

"But you're not going anywhere."

"I have no desire to go anywhere."

I was curious to meet a major figure in my world, sure, but I didn't feel any burning need to leave Milan. Right then and there, I was getting along fine with my team.

I walk on into the sweet Parisian night, a perfect opportunity to take a few steps back into the past, to remember. To remember one thing in particular: every time I've faced a serious decision as a coach, it's been challenging. They are always delicate situations. They can even verge on the comical. Like the time I took to my heels like a thief in the night, just to avoid signing a contract.

CHAPTER 4

Turkish Delights

Everything began in Istanbul, and from the very beginning I should have known that the city has a curse on it; that is, until someone proves otherwise. When I was relieved of my duties at Parma (June 1998, just as the second year in the three-year contract was up), the Turks showed up. Unlike the cliché, they didn't smoke. I did the smoking, actually. But they were generous with their money. Just three days after the final championship match, I heard from Fenerbahçe S. K., a team with twenty million fans, all of Asian Turkey at its feet. They really wanted me, that much was clear. The company that owned the team was well capitalized; the chairman, Aziz Yildirim, ran a high-end real estate company that ran Turkey's NATO bases. He was a dynamic and competent person, and at that moment I was his personal objective.

With one major sticking point: I really wasn't very excited about the idea.

They came to visit me at my home, and they wheedled a promise out of me: "All right, I'll come visit your training grounds for three days, without obligations. But the trip must be kept secret." Just like in Paris. The secret journey, which began with a flight in a private jet from Parma, continued this way: a triumphal welcome at Istanbul airport by thousands of Turkish fans, who actually carried me on their shoulders at one point. Accommodations in the imperial suite of the Hotel Kempinski, with a bathroom the size of an Olympic stadium. A constant procession of strangers bringing me carpets—so very many carpets. Dinner on the Bosphorus. An excursion on a sailboat, with photographers perched in the rigging. My name in banner headlines in every Turkish daily. Forty-eight hours of treatment befitting a Roman emperor—just the usual travel arrangements you make when you want to pass unobserved.

My last dinner in Istanbul was when they made their offer. "We'll give you three million dollars a season for three years." Translation: a lot of money. Just to put it in perspective: before then, Parma had been paying me 700 million lire ($550,000) a season, excluding bonuses (for the first year, 150 million lire ($120,000) if we won the Coppa Italia, 250 million lire ($200,000) for the UEFA Cup, and 500 ($400,000) for the Scudetto). All things considered, one fundamental truth is undeniable: Fenerbahçe S. K. was offering me a boatload of money.

But that wasn't what I was interested in. I'd only been coaching in Serie A for two years, not long enough to be able to risk stepping aside. I wanted to tell them no, but I had to figure out how. I had an idea: I'd keep raising my demands, until they got sick of it. "I want a villa on the beach."

Answer: Yes.

"I want a car with a driver."

Answer: Yes.

"You have to pay for all my air travel to and from Italy."

Answer: But of course.

"I pick my own technical staff and no one else has any say in it."

Answer: We wouldn't want it any other way.

"I beg of you, stop giving me carpets."

That was almost asking too much, but in the end they gave in on that point, too. Ask and you shall receive. Evidently, I'd chosen the wrong tactic. It was a total defeat on all fronts. My visit was really nothing more than a courtesy call, but Fenerbahçe was determined to get my signature on a contract, cost what it may. They seemed to be saying: "You're not leaving here until you sign our contract." A prisoner without bars—okay, but not great.

Luckily, even though I had been relieved of duty to make way for Alberto Malesani, my contract with Parma still had a year to run; that was what saved me. Or, at least, what saved me from lying. "I can't sign anything official right now. Let me go back to Italy, it'll only take me a few days to rescind my existing agreement, and then I'll come back to see you." That's what I said, but in my mind there was a rider: "As if." I managed to escape: Turkey– Emilia Romagna, a one-way ticket. There was just one thing left to do: inform Chairman Yildirim that, let us say, I had changed my mind. But I was too much of a chicken even for that: I had my wife call him and tell him on the phone. I was a little embarrassed at what I'd done.

Still, he wasn't giving up. He sent one of his emissaries to hunt me down, another one-way ticket: Istanbul to My House. The dreaded middleman Bilgiç arrived in Felegara by taxi while I was in my car, speeding back to Parma to keep from having to talk to him, like a thief in the night.

Was I crazy? No, it was much simpler than that. I was just the new coach of Juventus. How new? A couple of hours, to tell the truth. Blame it on a phone call from Luciano Moggi, which I don't think anyone wiretapped, that I received the day before I left on my little jaunt to Turkey. "Ciao, this is Luciano. I have to see you tomorrow."

"I can't do it tomorrow, I'm going to Istanbul."

"To do what?"

"There's a football club there that wants to see me."

"Before you commit to anything, I need to talk to you. Call me as soon as you get back . . ."

I figured he just wanted to talk to me about some player or other. As soon as I managed to elude the aggressive marking of the Turkish team, we made an appointment to meet the following day in Turin. That's right, you guessed it: a secret meeting. We were supposed to meet in front of the Hotel Principi di Piemonte, a car was waiting for me, and I fell in line behind it, following it until we reached the home of Antonio Giraudo. I was sitting across from Antonio Giraudo, Luciano Moggi, and Roberto Bettega. The Triad, before me in the flesh. They wasted no time coming to the point: "We want you to become the next coach for Juve."

"When would this be?"

"We know your contract with Parma still has a year to run, so from the coming season."

"Listen, though, don't you have Lippi? There's no one better than him."

"He's not happy, he's tired of being here, he's decided this is his last year. So we thought of you."

What did I think? I must have thought they were crazy and, as you know, it's dangerous to contradict the mentally unstable, so I went along with them. After a few more hours of conversation, they had me sign their contract. First impression: three reliable, competent individuals, three talented executives.

They wrote out the contract by hand on a sheet of letterhead stationery, blue ink on white paper, twenty-three lines in total, not including signatures. Here are a few passages:

1) Signore Carlo Ancelotti will take on, with the responsibilities of coach, the technical management and training of the first team of Juventus F. C. beginning with the 1999–2000 championship season until 30 June 2001.

2) For this position, Juventus F. C. will pay Signore Carlo Ancelotti the sum of Italian Lire 1,800,000 (one billion eight hundred million) [$1.5 million], net of withholding, for the soccer year of 1999–2000 and Italian Lire 1,800,000 (one billion eight hundred million) net of withholding, for the soccer year of 2000–2001.

3) Signore Carlo Ancelotti assigns to Juventus F. C. the right to exercise an option for the athletic year of 2001–2002 at the salary, established as of the signing of this contract, of Italian Lire 2,000,000 (two billion) [$1.6 million] […].

The numerical sums were written as shown above, missing a comma and three zeros, in millions, not billions: luckily, my bank account was safeguarded by the sums expressed in words, set in parentheses. Three signatures on the left and one signature on the right: Bettega and I signed with the same black ink, while Moggi and Giraudo signed in blue ink. I was going to be Lippi's successor; it was written on that sheet of paper.

I came home to Felegara, I summoned my family and friends, I was bursting with pride. Chest (and belly) protruding, I made the momentous announcement: "I'm the new Juventus manager." They shouted back in unison: "Oh, go take a shit—*va' a cagher*— you've lost your mind." After that, I had to carry the contract with me in my jacket pocket. I had accepted an offer from Juventus, valid from the start of the following year, and no one believed a word I said. As it turned out, I wound up on the Juventus bench earlier than scheduled, in February 1999: Lippi was having problems, but that is another story.

Every time I agreed to coach a new team, the decision was always accompanied by fireworks and occasionally by a mushroom cloud; in any case, it was never easy or simple. Except for the time I left Reggiana to go to Parma—I didn't have to think twice about that one. For that matter, from the Italian national team—where I was the assistant coach to the Maestro Arrigo Sacchi—to Reggiana, I gave up a safe perch for an uncertain future. Between Parma and Juventus, I was escaping the pressing tactics of the Turks.

Then came A. C. Milan in November 2001, and on that occasion I was fleeing the pursuit of Stefano Tanzi, who wanted to take me back to Parma. None of this is intentional, it just seems to happen to me; I move quicker than I mean to. Tanzi and I had a meeting on Friday and came to a verbal agreement; we agreed to meet at Parmalat headquarters the following Monday to get everything down in black and white. On Saturday, I rested up. On Sunday, I watched the Turin–Milan match on television with my old friend William Vecchi; and, to my surprise, I watched Stefano Tanzi announce on *Domenica Sportiva* that, beginning Tuesday, I was going to be his new coach. Every word was true. I guess Galliani was watching TV that Sunday, as well. On Monday morning, I took my son Davide to school; afterward I swung by Collecchio.

"I'm sorry, Carletto, you'll have to wait. Signore Tanzi is in a meeting. He'll be another hour or so."

"No problem, I'm going home; I only live ten minutes away. When he's free, give me a call and I'll come right over."

⌁

I was in the car when my cell phone rang, I thought it was Tanzi, but I was wrong: "Hello, this is Galliani. Ancelotti, where are you? Have you already signed the contract with Parma?"

"Not yet, but we're about to sign."

"Stop what you're doing, go home, lock the door and pull down the blinds. Wait for me. I'm on my way to your house, with Ariedo Braida. You have to come coach Milan, you're replacing Fatih Terim."

Oh, right. Here we go again. The first thing I did when I got home was unplug all the phones. They pulled up with the contract, and they talked me into it in thirty seconds flat. I signed on the kitchen table. I was there from 6 November 2001 to 30 June 2004. It was the beginning of a love affair, as well as a story of victories and successes. The second chapter in a crazy passage of history, after my time at Milanello as a player. And the cause of a tremendous temper tantrum, absolutely justified, on Tanzi's part.

Then there is the story of Real Madrid: me and Florentino Pérez, tortellini *y merengues*, but I'll tell that one later. I won't run away, I promise.

CHAPTER 5

The Pig Is Sacred.
And the Pig Can Coach.

I scarf food down like a horse, and no one is happier than me. The champion of Italy, Europe, and the world; just take me to a trattoria, stand back, and watch. No one else can come close. I don't care about the side dishes, the secret lies in the filling: inside of what I eat is what I really am. I'm a philosopher of ragù, with an idea befitting a Nobel laureate: it's not the salami that hurts you, it's the knife.

One evening at the San Siro, I was continuing to field Clarence Seedorf, and some of the fans in the stands were voicing their disagreement, one gentleman louder than the others: "Go back to Parma and pig out on tortellini."

"And you go fuck yourself."

He was screaming in Italian, and I replied in proper French.

I wasn't defending Seedorf, it's just that I can't stand by and watch someone insult a perfectly good plate of tortellini.

It takes me back to my childhood. I was born into a family of farmers, and it's my memory of Sunday supper. A classic. Tortellini was the specialty of that day, only and exclusively that day, a sacred moment dedicated to my family, the air of home. Clean air. We were poor but polite, I don't know if we were much to look at. Me, my sister Angela, papa Giuseppe and mamma Cecilia, grandpa Erminio (whom we called Carlino), and grandma Maria: the family grouped around the tureen full of steaming tortellini. Home and church, first Holy Communion and then Sunday supper, guests at one house or the other. Tortellini, wine, and pork, a blue-plate special that was free of charge. Pork, and lots of it, because that was what farm families ate where I come from. We raised pigs, took care of them for a year, slaughtered them in the heart of winter, and then stuffed ourselves on pork. It was good meat, we ate it 365 days a year, and no one ever had problems with cholesterol. In fact, if you ask me, they invented cholesterol later. What I'm trying to say is that if I think of a pig, I feel like I'm thinking of something nice, almost a sacred animal, like a cow in India, say, or else Zlatan Ibrahimović for an Inter fan.

That's not what the Juventus fans thought, though. I have a memory that comes back to me in a flash every so often. It was my very first week on the job in Turin, I was driving to the office, and in the middle of Piazza Crimea I saw an obelisk. Nice, very striking, but what I really noticed was the graffiti someone had spray-painted onto it: "A pig can't coach." *Cuminciom ben*, as they say in Turinese dialect—this is a nice beginning. Inside, waiting for me, were all the soccer hooligan leaders, summoned by Moggi: "You have to make peace with Ancelotti, you understand?" No, they didn't understand, it doesn't do a bit of good to explain anything to them, you'd just be wasting money on a tutor.

I played for A. S. Roma in the 1980s, and our adversary was Juve. I played for Milan, and our chief opponent was Juve. I coached Parma, and in the Italian championship for the Scudetto we played against Juve. They only know me, and can only see me, as an enemy. End of story. That wasn't going to change, and it never will. They're just a few miserable losers, a few bad apples, surrounded by a city full of wonderful people—but that's cold comfort. The middle finger that I raised in the general direction of the Curva Scirea (the notoriously violent section of the stands at the Stadio Delle Alpi in Turin) one evening, when I was the coach of Milan, was dedicated to them. They lacked imagination, it was always the same refrain: "A pig can't coach." It just annoys the hell out of me. It shows an intolerable lack of respect toward pigs.

Because a pig can coach. Definitely. And a pig can win, despite everything those hooligans might say, and in defiance of the much more likable skepticism of my two friends from Parma, diehard Juventus fans, and the first people I thought of after we won the Champions League final against Juventus at Old Trafford. God bless Shevchenko's last penalty kick in Manchester. I bought two salamis, gift wrapped them with a lovely bow, and delivered them in person, with a pair of handwritten dedications: "To you, the salami; to me, the *Coppa*." They laughed, they took it in the right spirit. Because they know me better than most. They understand the way I operate: I love to eat pork *coppa*, it's a delicious cold cut from home, and I eat it when I can, but in Italian the *Coppa* also means the championship cup, and any opportunity I see to win one, I take. And I do it with all the determination of my family, with a philosophy of life that comes from my homeland. Pork and tortellini: when it comes down to it, no matter what else happens, you always come around to the same point of departure.

If it hadn't been for the hard work of my mother and father—mamma and papa—I'd be no different from anyone else. In the old days, you had to sacrifice: you worked the land with your hands and a few tools; there was no farm machinery, the days were long, and the work was endless. What you sow you can only hope to harvest a year later. There was no instant gratification; you had to be patient, you couldn't lose heart when the going got tough.

They worked the real fields, I worked the soccer fields. Their season culminated in a harvest, my season aimed at a Scudetto, an Italian championship, or else a cup of one kind or another—maybe European, maybe World. Worlds apart, and yet not that different after all. I was raised by a couple of excellent coaches. The product that brought in the most money for them in the old days was milk, but they never saw the money until the dairy sold the finished cheese. It might take a year or even a year and a half. In the meantime, while you were waiting to be paid, you had to be patient and make sure you had resources to fall back on. The art of keeping your cool was essential, and I learned it from them. It was an art that came in handy when I was injured as a player, and it's been crucial to me as a coach countless times. It helps me to keep things on track when I have to manage a situation and keep from lashing out in anger—say if I'm being pressured by a player's attitude, or sniping from fans or the ownership, or else the taunts of the media. You have to stay sensible, or you're done for.

The way you handle a group is the way you are, deep down. I prefer to talk with my players, not shout at them—though, after certain games, it does happen. I feel like a member of the group, inside it, not above it or beneath it. If someone has a problem, they're welcome to vent. If someone is angry, they can ask for an explanation, even if in some cases there are no explanations for the decisions that have been made: it's easy to choose between a player who trains and a player who prefers not to; it's not so clear-cut when you are dealing with two footballers that have similar qualities and who both try equally hard. In situations of that kind, the smart thing is to keep your mouth closed. I'm not a father to my team, but I'm a friend, and I'm definitely a psychologist. I've never had any murderous interactions with my players; it's much more common for us all to laugh together.

In Dubai, during the winter retreat with Milan, everyone burst out laughing except for one player: Mathieu Flamini, victim of the Brigand Chief, a prank that's really a bastard. But a spectacular one. You pick someone to be the butt of the joke, and usually you try to pick someone with a chip on his shoulder—*oui*, Flamini—and then you construct a fairy tale around them. You have to explain it to all the others, one by one, and that was a task that took it out of me; first you tell the Italians, in Italian, then you tell the Brazilians, in pseudo-Italian, and then you tell Beckham, with grunts and gestures. The plot is always the same. I'm the narrator of a story, and the players all take roles. These roles include the king, the queen, the coachman, the assistant coachman, the royal guards, the brigands, and, of course, the brigand chief. After dinner, Gattuso comes over to where I'm sitting and says, "Come on, coach, let's play Brigand Chief. It's fun, and there are some new players who've never done it before."

I raise one eyebrow and look skeptical, which is something that comes naturally to me. "No, not that game again. Don't ask me to do Brigand Chief. I'm tired, I don't feel like it tonight."

All the others, in chorus: "Coach, coach, coach."

This is where it starts, that was the signal. "Okay, but this really is the last time."

I begin to explain the rules, but it's really just for Flamini's benefit, because he's the only one who doesn't know what's going on. There are parts to be assigned, one for every player. It all goes without a hitch, until it's time to choose the brigand chief. That's when the fun begins.

Now it's Gattuso's turn to pipe up: "Tonight I want to play the brigand chief."

Inzaghi jumps to his feet, his napkin tumbling to the floor: "Jesus, Rino, that's enough! You've already been the brigand chief once, tonight it's my turn."

Kaladze breaks in, furiously: "Oh, you're all a bunch of brown-nosers, let an outsider have some fun for once."

Okay, it's time for me to intervene: "Now, boys, calm down. Let's let one of the new recruits have a shot at it."

Kaladze: "I vote for Beckham."

Kaká: "But Beckham doesn't even speak Italian. How can he be the brigand chief?"

Then it's my turn again: "Oh, I'm fine with Beckham."

Everyone turns to look at Flamini. He turns red with fury and practically shouts: "Me, me, *I* want to be the brigand chief!"

He went for it. He swallowed it hook, line, and sinker.

Now the prank can begin: I start to tell the story. "Once upon a time, in a beautiful castle, there lived ..." Maldini, waving a fork in one hand: "A king."

"And of course this king is married to ..."

Borriello, with swishy enthusiasm: "The queen."

"Whenever the king and queen want to leave the castle, they ride in a carriage pulled by six beautiful horses, and holding the reins is the ..."

Kalac, both hands pulling imaginary reins as he rocks on his seat, cries: "The coachman!"

"But the coachman never rides alone, at his side is his trusted ..."

Abbiati, almost dancing with joy: "Assistant coachman!"

I stop for a second and reflect: these players are going to try to win the Italian championship. My God.

"All together, the king and the queen, the coachman and assistant coachman, have to drive through a dangerous dark forest, so they must be escorted by the ..."

Emerson, Pato, Kaká, Dida, Ronaldinho, and Seedorf all leap to their feet, waving knives and shouting in unison: "Royal guards!!"

"Because lurking in the forest are the ..."

Zambrotta, Bonera, Antonini, and Jankulovski, with napkins on their heads: "The brigands!!!"

"And these brigands are commanded by the ..."

Silence. Flamini slowly gets up from his chair and practically whispers: "The brigand chief."

"No, Mathieu, that's not how we do it. You have to give it a little more oomph, you have to say it loud, like Maldini."

We start over. "And these brigands are commanded by the..."

Flamini, a little louder: "*The brigand chief!*"

Maldini: "You really don't get it, do you? You have to shout! It! Out!"

And, as always, the third try is the one that works. "And these brigands are commanded by the..."

Flamini, red-faced, shouts furiously: "**THE BRIGAND CHIEF!**"

There's a brief pause. Then everyone stands up, from Beckham to Sheva. The roar is terrifying, the entire A. C. Milan team, in a single thunderclap of a voice: ". . . **WHO GIVES EVERYONE BLOWJOBS AND WIPES HIS MOUTH ON A LEAF!**" The silence is deafening. Gattuso practically faints. Mathieu Flamini (a wonderful person, a genuine team player) glares at me angrily. I can read his expression, I know what he's thinking: "A pig can't coach."

CHAPTER 6

Faking a Fake

Nils Liedholm could have been a coach; he could also have been a stand-up comedian. He decided to split the difference: he did theater, but his venue was the locker room. He was my first mentor and teacher; he might also have been my first Brigand Chief. He was a genuine chief, of real brigands; that is, us. *Roma, capoccia der monno infame*, to put it in Roman dialect—Rome, the capital of the world of villains—with Il Barone, as he was jocularly known, as its emperor and guide. He never raised his voice, but he taught plenty of useful lessons, especially useful to the young man I was at the time. He wore me down with technique. "Dribble," and I'd dribble. "Dribble with your right foot," and I'd dribble with my right foot. "Dribble with your left foot," and I'd dribble with my left foot. "Slalom dribble," and I'd pretend to be Alberto Tomba with a soccer ball. "Do a leg fake," and I'd start to stumble. "Fake a fake," and I'd fake it, pretending I'd actually understood what he'd said. In reality, though, I was delving deeply in an attempt to resolve a question that was tormenting me: "What the fuck is he talking about?"

He was an extraordinary person. He could make you laugh; at the same time, his profound calm and inner tranquility would astonish you. We were haunted by the fear of losing him; the odds were always highest when we played away games in Milan. The train left Rome's Termini station at midnight. That was far too late for him. He'd have someone drive him to the out-of-the-way station of Roma Tiburtina at ten o'clock, then he'd climb aboard a sleeper car sitting empty by the platform, get comfortable, and go to sleep. At eleven thirty, they'd hook the sleeper car to the rest of the train and then pull into the main station where we were all waiting, ready to set off on our journey of hope—a journey of hope, in the sense that we always hoped Liedholm was with us, that he hadn't been hooked onto the wrong locomotive, one heading for, say, Amsterdam or Reggio Calabria. Every time it was a crapshoot. The next morning, we'd tumble out of the train exhausted, stubble-faced, in Milan. The only one who looked rested was Liedholm, who could have slept through an atomic bomb. "Boys, how are we doing this morning?"

"Doing great, Coach."

And off we'd go to our hotel, to play cards and maybe set fire to our hotel room.

At the Grand Hotel Brun, in Milan's San Siro neighborhood, we once came mighty close to doing just that. It was the evening before the Inter–Roma match of 1981. After dinner, it was the usual group of us lying around in our room: me, Roberto Pruzzo, and Bruno Conti. Pruzzo was sprawled out comfortably on the bed, reading a copy of the *Corriere dello Sport*. A lightbulb clicked on in Conti's massive brain: actually, it was a Bic lighter that clicked into flame. In any case, that genius Conti crept over and set fire to the corner of Pruzzo's paper. Pruzzo saw the sudden burst of flame, promptly wet his pants, and threw the fiery stack of paper across the hotel room. It dropped to the floor at the bottom of the curtains, next to the bed. In no time the curtains were burning, too. It was an historic conflagration: if Nero had been there, he'd have been tuning his violin. The hotel staff were running up and down the stairwells in search of a fire extinguisher. At last, with much huffing and puffing, they managed to put out the flames in the hotel room, and then the ones all over Conti. Conti paid for the damages to the hotel room, but he never bought Pruzzo another copy of that day's *Corriere dello Sport*.

We felt a breath of freedom thanks to Liedholm. With freedom, however, came a number of things; once, a trip to the hospital for the whole team. We left for an away game and wound up on gurneys. We were scheduled to travel to Avellino, near Naples, for the Coppa Italia, and the schedule was routine: practice in the morning, lunch together at Trigoria, departure. Unfortunately, we were running early that day, and our coach had a brilliant idea. We dropped by to watch our archrivals Lazio play at the Stadio Flaminio. "Come on, boys, it's on the way . . ." *Li mortacci sua*, as they say in Rome: "Curse his ancestors and forebears." We were going to pay a call on Lazio.

We showed up without calling ahead but—how can I put this?—we didn't manage to slip into our seats unnoticed. We were a glaring yellow-and-red stain on the enemy's best carpet. The die-hard fans noticed us and gave us the warm welcome they reserve for their crosstown cousins: "*Merde!* Pieces of shit!" The whole stadium turned to stare and shout toward the stands where we were sitting. We sat there, uncomfortably, for eighty minutes; we tried to leave, unobtrusively, ten minutes before the end of the match. The team bus was parked about two hundred yards from the ground. Liedholm was friends with a couple of Rome city cops, and he just climbed into the backseat of their police wagon. We, on the other hand, were left to our own devices. We tiptoed down the stadium stairs, walked out into the parking lot, and there was the entire population of the Lazio fan club, waiting to say hello. So thoughtful of them. We started walking toward the bus, and jackbooted kicks began to fly. We sped up, and vicious insults filled the air. We broke into a run, and legs stuck out to trip us up. It was a full-fledged mob attack—not our idea of fun. Everything imaginable was flying through the air in our general direction, and, for the first time, I put the Maestro's teachings into practice. "Dribble with your right foot," and I gave a Lazio fan a sharp kick in the ass. "Dribble with your left foot," and I let fly with another vigorous kick in the ass. "Slalom dribble," and I avoided a couple of *biancazzurri*. "Do a leg fake," and I faked my way past two more Lazio hooligans. "Fake a leg fake," and I did my best to pretend I wasn't dying. We had a rough time of it in that parking lot, but we finally made it back to the team bus. It really should have come as no surprise, but still we were horrified to discover that Liedholm hadn't made it back yet. They picked up rocks from the ground and threw them at us, smashing the bus windows. Some of the team were hurt by this point, and blood had begun to flow. There was nothing we could do but try to lie low, on the floor of the bus, in the aisle running between the seats. It was a little corner of hell. Finally, out of nowhere, Liedholm showed up, not a hair out of place, escorted by two city cops.

"Why, boys, what's happened to the bus? Why are you lying on the floor?"

We explained everything to him in chorus: "Go fuck yourself."

He was a character. A phenomenon. Before every major match he would instruct Dr. Ernesto Alicicco to tell us jokes in the locker room. But that afternoon, we were the joke ourselves, and the punch line didn't make us laugh. So the Roma team walks into the Lazio stadium . . . In the emergency room, we got so many stitches we could have run up a whole new set of team uniforms with the thread.

Roma was just that way. My nickname on the team was Il Bimbo—the Kid—and Il Bimbo is who I am. Someday, I'm going to coach that team, I have a debt of gratitude. It was a fun team to play for. From the very first day. From back in 1979, when Liedholm, on his way back home from a holiday at the spa in Salsomaggiore with his wife, stopped by to see me in Parma and took me away with him. The transfer fee was 1.2 billion lire ($950,000). It was like an episode of *The Price Is Right*. And, from the minute I got there, it was clear that I was in a unique place, and first impressions matter.

I got off the train from San Benedetto del Tronto at Rome's Termini station with simple, easy-to-follow instructions: "Get a taxi outside the station, tell him to take you to Via del Circo Massimo, the press conference is being held there. Pay close attention: a yellow taxi, with writing on the door and TAXI written on the dome light on the roof; don't take a gypsy cab, they'll charge extra." Fine. I obeyed the instructions to the letter, but the taxi driver didn't recognize me; we pulled up outside of Roma headquarters, and there was a screaming, chanting crowd of four thousand delirious fans. In fact, the transfer season of 1979 was an important time: Turone and Benetti had just arrived, Conti had returned from being on loan, and Romano had joined in defense. It was a nice feeling, I felt like one of the team. I was ready to get out of the cab, asked the driver how much I owed him. "Ten thousand lire." I pulled out my wallet, extracted a ten thousand lire note, handed it to him. There was a growl of disapproval from the fan base. When they saw that I was paying the cabbie, the crowd turned ugly, and insults flew in the general direction of that unfortunate taxi driver. "A Lazio fan!" "Dirty traitor!" "*Nun te devi fa' paga'*—don't take his money!" "*Cojone*, asshole, Roma is sacred!" To make a longish story short, they hemmed the cab in, taking the driver hostage, and started rocking the car back and forth for no good reason—and with me inside. I started feeling seasick. It must be fate—I seem to remember the faces of a lot of taxi drivers. He was terrified: "Get out. The ride is free. *Just get out of my cab. Beat it!*" My career was just beginning, and they were already ordering me out of taxicabs.

There was just one minor detail: I still didn't have a signed contract. With Parma, I was earning ten million lire ($8,000) a year; now that Roma had recruited me, I had decided to ask them for a hundred million. I was at the summer training camp in Brunico, we'd been working for a few days, so I went to talk directly with the chairman, Dino Viola, a magnificent manager and leader, and a man who counted pennies. "Ancelotti, how much do you want?"

"A hundred million lire a year, Mister Chairman."

"You are out of your mind."

Then three weeks of total silence. On the last working day before the regular season began, Viola himself called me: "Ancelotti, have you thought about your salary?"

"Well, maybe we could talk it over . . ." So I let him talk me down to 24 million lire ($20,000) a year before taxes, from my original demand of 100 million lire a year after taxes. Twenty-four million lire—more or less the same salary Parma had been paying me. How long did negotiations last? About twenty-nine seconds. Results of the negotiations: disastrous. Just like my debut in Serie A, at the Stadio Olimpico, playing against the champions of Italy, A. C. Milan. Enormous tension, enormous excitement, an unsettling sense of doubt as to whether I was up to the challenge of that gigantic world. After the first minute of play, Conti runs up the length of the pitch and hits the post, Pruzzo brings it down with his head. I'm in the penalty area, Albertosi makes a miraculous save, and the ball rolls out half a meter in front of me. I can't believe my luck—on my début in Serie A! I close my eyes, pull back, and send an intercontinental missile toward the goal; so hard my foot was hurting afterwards. Albertosi gets to his feet and blocks the ball with his face. Jesus, he blocks it with his *face*. The ball ricocheted away from the goal—final score: 0–0. I was confused, a little angry, but almost happy. Deep inside, part of me was celebrating. I finally understand, I've finally learned. I faked a fake. I faked a goal.

CHAPTER 7

Achilles' Knee

Peppe didn't need to fake anything. He really was on the verge of dying on the spot, of a massive myocardial infarction—heart attack, to the layman. If he did, we already had our stories straight: we would just blame it on Bruno Conti. The situation was appropriate; there he stood, wrapped in toilet paper, ready to be flushed away if necessary.

Peppe was in charge of the team warehouse; he'd been hired by A. S. Roma after he appeared on the playing field one day. It was a Roma–Inter match, Inter had a last-minute penalty shot, and Peppe had been unable to restrain himself. He hopped over the fence at the Stadio Olimpico. Howling like a madman, he'd rushed forward, but it had ended badly for him: beaten silly in front of five thousand screaming fans. The team owners wanted to save him from similar embarrassments in the future, so they took pity and gave him a job in the warehouse. He was a tiny little guy, a hard worker, with a very odd tic: he'd stick out his tongue and blow, then fake a dry spit. It was a brilliant masterpiece of weirdness, which always culminated the same way, with the same phrase repeated twice: "Up Lazio's ass, up Lazio's ass." And who could argue with that sentiment?

One evening at training camp, we decided to play a prank on him. Me, Roberto Pruzzo, and Roberto Scarnecchia took Conti and wrapped him in toilet paper. Rolled from head to toe: he was so little that it only took a few rolls. "Soft, strong, and very long— Bruno Conti." He really looked like a mummy; we even dabbed on a couple of spots of Mercurochrome to give him that nice dried-blood effect. At two in the morning, we stood him right outside of Peppe's room, knocked on the door, and ran like the wind. When the poor little guy opened the door, Conti let out an infernal howl: "*Mwah-hah-hah-hah*." Peppe gasped and staggered backward, the prank had worked perfectly. A little too perfectly, in fact: he had turned pale. He was mouthing words, but no sound was coming out. He was paralyzed by fear. "Peppe, it's only me, Bruno." Maybe that's what really scared him . . . Anyway, we had to call a doctor. A couple of quick slaps in the face, and he was fine.

I considered kneeling down to beg forgiveness, but then I decided against it: "Right, smart boy, you'll never get back up." Achilles had weak heels, Pinocchio and Tassotti had spectacular noses, I had my knees: let's just say that they weren't exactly my strong point. I found out how weak my knees were when I was playing for Roma, with two serious on-field injuries. I don't have the strongest memory where dates are concerned, but October 25

1981 is a day I'll always remember. We were playing Fiorentina, and Francesco Casagrande—a determined halfback who had already broken my nose once when he was playing for Cagliari—was marking me. While I was trying to pivot to reach a throw-in, I made a strange move after chesting the ball down. I'd twisted my knee, and my teammates all took it out on him: "Bastard." In fact, though, he hadn't done a thing wrong; the instant replay on RAI television was crystal clear, he'd never even touched me.

The things that flood into your mind in those few seconds are crazy. The first thing that came to mind was Francesco Rocca, aka Kawasaki, an idol of mine, my first roommate when I came to play for Roma. In my mind, I reviewed his slow recovery, a lengthy period of torment after a serious injury, and, more importantly, I tasted the fettuccine (pansful at a time) that his mamma used to make for us in San Vito Romano after each training session. To tell the truth, I remembered the fettuccine first, then I remembered my teammate (after all, life is about priorities). Anyway, I had just ruptured my anterior cruciate ligament, but, since my menisci were still sound, we decided to try to recuperate without surgery. I stayed off my leg for a month, then I got back on my feet, and I was put on the bench for a game against Napoli. The next day, side-footing the ball during training with the youth team, I heard a distinct *clock* sound from inside my knee. Come again? *Clock.* Oh, thanks, now I understand perfectly. Two sharp sounds, and my knee was bent permanently. I was in Trigoria, I lay down on my sofa, and I called Doctor Alicicco. "Ernesto, something's wrong. I think I broke my meniscus."

"No, I doubt that very much."

"Please come take a look."

"I'm on my way."

He was checking me over, increasingly confident that it wasn't my meniscus: "See, it can't be your meniscus; this is the meniscus over here," and as he spoke he lightly touched the spot with one finger. I leapt straight into the air, I hate to admit it. Still, even back then, I was already right one hundred percent of the time.

I underwent surgery, and recuperation was pure hell. Nowadays, just two months after surgery, Gattuso is already running; back then, two months after the operation, I swore like a sailor every time I tried to move. For forty-five days I was in a cast, in bed, with my leg at a forty-five-degree angle, in traction; then, for another month, I was in an air cast (a removable cast, which I took off every morning for physical therapy), followed by another thirty days during which I could only set my foot down lightly on the floor. Total time out of commission: one hundred and fifty days off my feet, no end of boredom and irritation, and an incredible array of pains. In the meantime, Rocca had stopped playing, but, since he was now an expert in the field of hobbling and limping, he stayed on with A. S. Roma, assigned to work on my recovery.

While bedridden, I actually put on some weight. I know—incredible . . . me, of all people! So Francesco decided to put me on a diet. During summer training camp, I worked separately with him while the team exercised and practiced. Every morning, he put me on the scale, and I never lost a pound. Nothing. It drove him crazy. He couldn't figure it out.

"Why aren't you losing weight? Carletto, what am I doing wrong?"

"Francesco, I don't understand it either. But it's got to be your fault."

If he took the blame, credit went to the fans. In Brunico, not all the players slept in the main wing of the hotel. Many of us were housed in an annex where each room had a kitchen of its own. Fans would bring us wild mushrooms, we got hungry at a certain time of the evening, and at midnight we started cooking up *fettuccine ai funghi*. If those mushrooms had been poisonous, today Rome would have just one soccer team. We ate epic quantities of pasta. I finally recovered completely in October 1982, round as a soccer ball but happy, just in time to begin the preseason leading up to the Scudetto and skip the World Cup entirely. "Champions of the World. Champions of the World. Champions of the World." They were. I would only become a champion later, with A. C. Milan.

And to think that Enzo Bearzot would have taken me to Spain. I had already debuted in the Italian national team in January 1981, in Montevideo, Uruguay, when Italy played the Netherlands. I played in the Mundialito; I scored a goal after six minutes of play, and I even won a gold watch that the organization put up as a prize. My teammates, the older ones especially, took that outcome with wisdom and philosophy: "Lucky jerk."

After the match, I went out to celebrate with Marco Tardelli and Claudio Gentile, and then we went to dinner. Of course, we got back late. My first thought, as we returned to the hotel: "I'm with Tardelli and Gentile, so there's no problem." My second thought, as I saw Bearzot waiting for us at the lobby doors: "No problem, my ass."

I was the ass, and my time was up. We went around to the back entrance, we took the elevator, we punched 3 for our floor.

The elevator doors slid open; we were home free—or almost. We would have been, too, if it hadn't been for that tiny detail: Bearzot, waiting to greet us. *Il Vecchio*—the Old Man—in person: "You two, Tardelli and Gentile, you can go. But I'm surprised at you, Ancelotti." A few sharp words and he was gone. I felt horrible. I was pale as a sheet. I went mum, didn't feel like saying a word. I was frozen motionless in shock. I would gladly have thrown myself at his feet, on my knees, begging for forgiveness. All familiar symptoms that my teammates had seen before. Conti, a few yards down the hall, was laughing. It was a good thing he wasn't dressed up as a mummy.

CHAPTER 8

A Dog,
Champion of Italy

Rome, a city of madness, the capital of my heart. I don't know a thing about Milan, but I know everything about Rome. It was there that I learned to live, even though my relationship with my finest moments is a strange one: I don't remember much about them. In soccer, as in life—even private life—the things that really stick with you are your disappointments, and I'm not all that interested in talking about them. The 1983 Scudetto was my first victory, but all that remains in my head are a few snapshots. And not all that many, to tell the truth. A. S. Roma, champions of Italy for the first time in forty years, and I can rest on those laurels; there are places where I'm still treated like a king. We used to eat frequently at Da Pierluigi, in Piazza de' Ricci, and, even today, if I dine there I might as well leave my wallet at home. They won't let me pay; a Scudetto is forever.

In the crucial period of the season, we played a home match against Juventus, our biggest rivals for the Scudetto, and we lost. Michel Platini pulled a move a few minutes before the final whistle, Brio headed it in. Our five-point lead shrank to three, I'll admit we started wetting our pants, but Brio received his just deserts. A policeman's dog bit him in the tunnel, which was the very least that could have happened to him. It was a moment of high tension; people were talking and shouting, there was a general hubbub, some of the voices were angry: the German shepherd lost his temper. Sergio Brio wasn't really very popular with the rest of us players; he was too determined on the field, he could be a little vicious. After the victory, he was leaping in the air, shouting, laughing. That poor dog saw a giant ogre celebrating, and he got scared. He went straight for the butt cheek and bit him in the ass. What a remarkable thing it was. We carried the dog in triumph on our shoulders. I may be a little off center, but when I think about the Scudetto, that's the first image that comes into my head.

Then came the celebrations. We were returning to Rome from Genoa, where we had played the deciding match. The Appian Way was jammed solid, from Ciampino Airport to the center of the city. People were waiting for us as we pulled through in the team bus, it was just incredible. There was a symphony of car horns. They kept the decorations up in the streets for four or five months; we had given the city an excellent reason not to bother working. Cappuccino, breakfast pastry, and *Forza, Roma*. The first night, I put on a scarf, a cap, and a pair of dark glasses so as to pass unrecognized,

I hopped on my scooter and zipped around the city for hours. It's a wonderful place, and it's hard to win for precisely that reason— it's a city that reacts disproportionately both to the good things and the bad things. It isn't easy to keep your equilibrium in a place like that, but it remains a one-of-a-kind city.

A Roma fan is more versatile than others; he has a distinctive sense of humor. I love to listen to people from Rome when they talk; they come up with unforgettable wisecracks. Once, when I was already playing for A. C. Milan, we played an away game in Rome. At the Stadio Olimpico, construction was underway for the 1990 World Cup, so we went over to the Stadio dei Marmi to warm up. People were allowed in to watch, and comments of all hues and shades were flying. Pietro Paolo Virdis emerged from the locker room with his unmistakable mustache, reminiscent of the little man on the Bialetti espresso pots. One of the Roma fans yells out: "Hey, Moka Express." I thought that was fantastic. I still can't see Virdis without smelling the coffee. Another time, just before a Roma–Juventus match, Brio emerged from the tunnel into the stadium. Yes, the famous Sergio Brio, aka Sergione (Big Sergio), but without a German shepherd's teeth clamped into his butt cheek this time. Instead, he had Rui Barros right next to him. Brio was six foot three, Rui Barros was five foot four. They were a sight to behold. From the crowd, the voice of a modernist poet floated over the field. "Hey, Brio, *ma che te sei portato*? What'd you bring with you? Your lighter?" Followed by ninety-two minutes of laughter and applause.

I didn't get any applause, though, when I got hurt the second time. It was worse than the first time, and now it was my left knee.

In December 1983, champions of Italy, we were playing against Juventus in Turin. I jumped to head a long ball, Cabrini was behind me, and he put one hand on my shoulder, knocking me slightly off balance. I landed wrong on my left knee. *Clock*. What? *Clock*, again? That's right, *clock*. Now my knee was talking to me, and the news wasn't good. Once again, I couldn't control the lower half of my leg, just like the first time. It was a bad feeling—all over again. Another operation, with surgery by Professor Perugia; more physical therapy, with Silio Musa. After six months, I still couldn't extend my leg. Professor Perugia had found some adhesions: "I'm sorry about this, but we're going to have to do another minor procedure. It's called a 'manipulation under anaesthesia.'" I didn't like the sound of that; I got a shiver down my spine. "Maybe you should perform a manipulation under anesthesia on your sister, Professor." Just to make sure that I felt as bad as possible, they gave me an appointment for a clinical visit the day after the final game of the Champions Cup, which we lost in Rome against Liverpool. What that meant, in practical terms, was that they saved the cost of the anesthesia, even though I'd only watched the match from the stands. I hobbled into Villa Bianca, and they all acted happy to see me: "Back again, Carletto? What a pleasure to have you here." They were sincerely happy, too, but I told them all to go to hell just the same. They put my leg in a cast, fully extended, the foot twisted to one side. It hurt like crazy. In the end, though, I got better.

Around the same time, another player for Roma, Paolo Giovannelli, was injured. He was a friend. Unlike me, he had torn his posterior cruciate ligament. The same thing happened to him: after six months, he still wasn't better, he still hadn't regained complete freedom of movement in that leg. So he heard the doctor utter a phrase I knew all too well: "We're going to have to do a manipulation under anaesthesia." At that point, the ears of Professor Perugia's sister must have started ringing, just as I was beginning to ask myself some questions: "So, if I had to be put in a cast with my leg extended in order to recover complete freedom of extension, what are they going to do to him so he can recover the ability to bend his leg?" Well, it was surprisingly simple. They trussed it up. They put him to sleep, manipulated the leg, wrapped it, and tied it. It looked like a giant salami. I took one look at it and heard my stomach rumble with hunger. My immediate impulse was to eat it, but my sense of friendship held me back. He was howling like a wild animal, so I just made fun of him: "Oh, you're just a giant baby, there's no such thing as pain."

I wasn't kidding, pain really doesn't exist. It's only a theory I have, but it seems to work. Knees are just enemies we have to fight; the war started years ago and continues today. I want to run, my head tells me I have to go, I go, my knee swells up, but I ignore it. It's the knee that's suffering, not me or my mind. It bothers the knee for me to run, there are no menisci anymore, so running is a lot harder on it, but I refuse to give up. My knees have made me suffer a lot over the years, now it's my turn. So I punish them, often running through the woods, uphill and down. Or else I run on a treadmill or on hard surfaces; oh, how it hurts them. And the more they swell up, the harder I run; it serves them right. Every so often I talk to them, I insult them. There are even times when I take offense and refuse to talk to them. Maybe I belong in an insane asylum, but if that's where I wind up I'm fine with it, because my knees are going in with me. I can already imagine the newspaper headlines: "Carletto Defeated By Nonexistent Pain." And the interview with Brio: "Then what was that pain I felt in my butt cheek?"

All kidding aside, it's an excellent psychological exercise. Challenges and difficulties aren't obstacles: you can and you must go beyond them. Aside from my second injury, there was Sven-Göran Eriksson, who had, in the meantime—June 1985—replaced Liedholm in the dugout. He was young, Swedish, and he had already won the UEFA Cup with I. F. K. Gothenburg; he had just come to Italy from Portugal, and you couldn't understand a word he said in Italian, practically the same as now. "*Tre muuuu tre.*" At first, some people thought he was saying "three times three" and they'd answer: "Nine?" Then it dawned on us that he was trying to say "three against three." We played a lot of practice matches, *tre muuuu tre,* and later *quattro muuuu quattro.*

Eriksson brought a whole new way of working to the team; he prepared meticulously, he was respectful, and he was good-hearted and open to helping the players. Every morning, when he came to work, he would go around and shake hands with all the players, until finally there were some who couldn't take it anymore, like Pruzzo. Eriksson would extend his hand, Pruzzo would reach out and shake it, saying: "A pleasure to meet you, I'm Roberto."

I was pretty comfortable, even if, during that period, I began to understand just what it meant to be benched. I had recovered from my injury, but he wouldn't let me play; he believed in Stefano Desideri and Giuseppe Giannini, both of whom had come out of the youth league. I felt that I had been sidelined, I thought he was overlooking me or that he had it in for me. That wasn't the case at all; he put me back on the first team, and the following year he even offered to make me captain, because Agostino Di Bartolomei had moved over to A. C. Milan and Conti didn't want to take on that level of responsibility. Me—captain of Roma. I represented a team and three-quarters of the city, because, let's admit it, there really aren't that many Lazio fans in Rome.

Right before one game, we walked into the locker room in I can't remember which stadium, and we were suddenly hit with a serious wave of nausea. It was a stink the likes of which none of us had ever encountered before. Ciccio Graziani hurried over to the toilets and, with his usual savoir faire attempted delicately to determine who was behind that stench: *"Ahò, ma che te sei magnato? I ratti der Tevere?"* Roughly translated: "What have you been eating, rats from the Tiber?" A door swung open, and Eriksson emerged, red-faced. "Relax, boys. It's just the coach who's crapped his pants." Like Liedholm, he never lost his temper. He was Liedholm's natural successor. He really was a great coach. One of the reasons that my relationship with Roma cooled considerably was the team's decision to get rid of Eriksson in April of 1987. The previous year, we had lost a spectacular championship match for the Scudetto, the famous game against Lecce, even though we had played beautifully. *Undici muuuu undici*—eleven against eleven.

CHAPTER 9

"Hello, This Is Silvio. I Want to Win Everything There Is to Win."

They made me sick of being part of that team. I lost my enthusiasm for the club, my passion for playing there withered and died. All kinds of odd things were going on, but most importantly, A. S. Roma had just bought two players—Lionello Manfredonia and Rudi Völler. They'd overspent, and it was time to sell a player to make up the difference. The only player anyone wanted to buy was me. A martyr to a fallen market.

In 1987, A. C. Milan hired a young coach named Arrigo Sacchi, and for some reason or another he was obsessed with putting me on the team. He wanted me at all costs, even more than he wanted Ruud Gullit and Marco van Basten, who had already been bought by other teams. I was ticked off, I wanted the deal to go through right away, but I had to cool my heels; it was ratified on the last day of the transfer period. I was at the beach in Sardinia; the secretary general of A. S. Roma, Roberto Borgogno, called me: "You've been sold. Come back to Rome, I'll give you an address, and you can go and meet with an executive from A. C. Milan."

Palazzo al Velabro. That was the address he gave me. It was a residential hotel in the historic center of Rome. I went straight over, walked in, my curiosity aroused. The concierge didn't say a word; he just handed me the key to the room and gave me a quick wink. Right then and there, I couldn't guess why. It became clear afterwards. I went upstairs, opened the door, and walked into a vast reception room. On the table was a nice little spread: champagne and finger pastries. I left the alcohol alone, but I ravaged the trayful of pastries, leaving only crumpled paper wrappers. Unexpectedly, out of nowhere, an A. C. Milan executive popped into the room; he looked young and vigorous, but there wasn't a hair on his head. Not a single, blessed hair; I know, I checked carefully. This was Adriano Galliani, the managing director of the club. Also known as Lo Zio—Uncle Adriano. I thought back to the winking concierge. I put myself in his position, behind the reception desk, and it all made sense. In comes a bald gentleman who asks for champagne and a tray of finger pastries to be delivered to room such-and-such, then he sees me arrive, Carletto, aka Il Bimbo— the Kid, and ask for the keys to that same room. Now I understand the wink: he thought we were lovers.

This was the first time I'd ever met Galliani. We talked about his philosophy, the team, and what he hoped to accomplish: "We have great ambitions." That was a phrase I'd already heard a thousand times before. "We want to win the Italian championship next year, and play in the UEFA European championship; we want to win the UEFA Cup in two years, and in the third year we want to win the Intercontinental Cup." Okay, that's something I haven't heard. I took a look at my watch. This guy is talking like he's drunk, but it's too early in the day to think he's guzzled that much hard liquor. Maybe he's just lost his mind. A short while later, I found myself on the phone with Silvio Berlusconi. For the first time. "*Pronto?* Yes, this is the chairman."

"*Buon giorno.*"

"*Buon giorno* to you. How are your knees?"

He wasn't exactly beating around the bush. He came straight to the point, with his first question.

"Mr. Chairman, my knees are fine."

"Well, we're counting on you. We want to win the Italian championship next year, in two years we want the Champions' Cup, and, for the third year, we want the Intercontinental Cup."

Okay, now it's official. Everyone's drunk. What the hell did they put in the water up in Milan? He was funny, though, joke after joke; it was invigorating to talk to him. "*Arrivederci*, then, Mr. Chairman."

"*Arrivederci*, Carletto. Let's keep our fingers crossed; we don't want any unpleasant surprises from your physical."

I crossed my fingers, and touched my balls to ward off evil while I was at it.

No question about it, that physical was going to be a crucial rite of passage. It was me against my knees, my old archenemies. The following day, the A. C. Milan team physician, Monti, flew down to Rome. Actually, the physical examination was performed by Professor Perugia, the surgeon who had operated on my knees. I have to say that Monti expressed serious misgivings about my knees. Despite his doubts, the team accepted me.

My journey from Trigoria to Milanello was a voyage to a different planet. And when I landed on that planet, I met someone who struck me as insane at first: Arrigo Sacchi. Before long, though, it dawned on me that Sacchi was a genius, not a madman. Truly a great man. Another mentor, another maestro. My first training sessions with him were challenging, to say the least. Usually I spend the time between soccer seasons exercising and training. That summer, instead, since I knew I was being let go, I just lay around and relaxed. I was in terrible shape, and my first warm-up with Arrigo was a terrible experience. His methods were completely innovative. Let's say that the benchmark for intensity of training had been twenty. Well, at Milanello the level of intensity was a solid hundred. There was just a world of difference, a tremendous and exhausting challenge. At the end of the day, we were all terrified at the thought of climbing the stairs to our bedrooms; we couldn't face it. Grown men though we were, we broke down sobbing. It was an ordeal, we moved like a squadron of zombies. The short walk from the dining hall to the locker room was a struggle of the will: "We *will* go out for training . . . we *can't* go out for training . . ." In the end, of course, we always went out for training; in fact, the pace only increased. The problem was that the day wasn't over at seven in the evening, after our second training session. Then it was time for dinner, and after an espresso (and before we were allowed to go to bed), Sacchi held a team assembly. Not a technical meeting, a psychological meeting. There was a psychologist named

Bruno De Michelis and another executive, a man named Zaccuri, who was director of human resources for Fininvest, Berlusconi's holding company. De Michelis: "Give me a list of fifty objects, and I'll write them on this blackboard, numbering them from one to fifty." The first thing that came into everyone's mind: "Okay, so they're crazy, not us." We decided to humor them, and began listing objects: loaf of bread, house, football, bowl of tortellini (guess who came up with that one), goal, stadium, pussy, car, cup of coffee, and so on, until we'd named fifty objects. De Michelis: "Now I'm going to turn the blackboard around, and I'm going to name them all, in order, without looking." He did it, too: loaf of bread, house, soccer ball, bowl of tortellini, goal, stadium, pussy, car, cup of coffee . . . He didn't miss a single one. "Now I'll repeat all the words in reverse order: cup of coffee, car, pussy, stadium, goal, bowl of tortellini, soccer ball, house, loaf of bread." Incredible. We thought we were smarter than him, we weren't about to let him get away with it.

"Pardon me, Doctor, but what was number thirty again?"

"Sheet of paper."

What about number twenty? "Pen."

And number forty-seven? "Sofa."

New lesson: the brain can do an amazing number of things. Every night, after two daily training sessions, that's what we did for an hour and a half. Then we started learning relaxation techniques. We would attain a state of complete relaxation through music and words. First we studied the theory of relaxation, and then we'd put it into practice. We'd listen to a piece of music, usually the theme song from *Chariots of Fire*, with the lights turned down low.

De Michelis and Zaccuri would talk over the theme music: "Now, relax your body, listen to your heartbeat. Imagine that you're on the soccer field, you see the stadium full of fans, the match is about to begin, you smell the aroma of the grass." They were like a couple of celebrity hypnotists. I still use their techniques today when I'm in a stressful situation. The first team member to collapse was usually Francesco Zanoncelli. He didn't just fall asleep, he fainted. We could have stuck a fork in him, he was so cooked. By the end of the relaxation session, half the team was sleeping.

So that was A. C. Milan, the team that was scheduled to win the Italian Scudetto this year, the UEFA Champions' Cup the next season, and the Intercontinental Cup the third season. *Sem mis ben*, as the Milanese would say: We're all set. When they turned the lights back on, we'd pick up Zanoncelli's lifeless body and head upstairs to bed. When training began, I weighed 84 kilos (185 pounds); by the time it was done, I was down to 78 kilos (171 pounds). After training camp, I went back home. I knocked at the door, and my own mother didn't recognize me. There was a stranger at the door. "What have they done to you? Look at you, you're just skin and bones ..."

Psychologically, we were becoming powerhouses. Part of it was the sheer challenge of tolerating Arrigo Sacchi. He'd explain game plans at night, just as you were falling asleep. He'd sketch them out on the door of your room. He was especially priceless when he had to explain strategy to Gullit and van Basten, who spoke no Italian. In that case, the fallback was English, which made it hard to keep a straight face. When we had to sit through the first meetings in English, it was pure torture to keep from laughing out loud. To avoid snorting, or just bursting into hilarity, we would pretend to clear our throats. Me and Tassotti started, and soon everyone was doing it. *"Its nesessari tu ev a sciort tim"*: if I had to write it down in black and white, that's how it looked to me, as an Italian. It's necessary to have a short team. *"Uen de boll arraivs, uan go e uan cam."* When the ball arrives, one go and one come. It truly was impossible to understand.

Everything sort of culminated just before a friendly match in Parma. Technical pregame meeting: oh, Lord, sense of terror, what's he going to say now? What are we supposed to do? We walked into the meeting room, there was a pillar in the middle of the room, all twenty-two of us clustered behind it, trying to hide; if we broke into laughter, how would he ever know? This was the first pillar in the history of the world to possess forty-four legs, in lines of six, with two left over. Sacchi was practically talking to himself, blathering on in English. We couldn't take it anymore, so we leveled with him: "Coach, your English totally sucks."

He was number one, the best and the loudest. Even when he was sleeping. He didn't dream, he screamed and shouted. While he was sleeping, he emitted terrifying sounds, as if someone were trying to cut his throat. Every so often, there would be a technical comment as well, even while he was fast asleep: "Run diagonaaalllll, diagonaaalllll!!!" or else, "go back, go back, go back, **GOOOO BAAAACCCKKKK!**" Jesus, the man never stopped. It was the secret of his success, and perhaps the source of great misery—to him and to others.

Before slipping into his nightly cataleptic trance, around ten thirty, he'd make the circuit of the players' bedrooms. He shuffled along in his slippers, we could hear him coming. We switched off the lights, jumped into bed, covered our heads with our blankets, and pretended we were sleeping. Daniele Massaro was the worst, he always did it. We thought—and said—terrible things about Sacchi at first; that is, until he finally obtained the level of play he was looking for. It wasn't really clear what we would have achieved without his maniacal dedication to his work. Certain techniques weren't natural; it was just inhuman how hard we practiced. One diagram after another, one play after the next. A relentless schedule of tactical exercises. He always told me: "You like to run, and you do a lot of running. But I want something more: I want you to become a conductor, with the team as your orchestra. You need to study music, tempo. We are performing a symphony, and you need to know every note by heart." The tempo, the time, was made up of: stop the ball and pass the ball. Stop and pass. Stop and pass. Every so often, just to let off steam, I'd add a little touch of my own: stop without passing, in the sense that Sacchi would stop practice entirely and tell me to start over from the beginning. We practiced for hours, me and him on our own, doing the simplest things. Things out of soccer preschool. Could we try dribbling now and then? No, stop and pass. Stop and pass. In the end, I knew exactly what I needed to do; he'd taught me perfectly. He showed me how to be relaxed and confident. I possessed a series of standard movements; I knew exactly where I needed to go when Tassotti had the ball, or Maldini or Baresi or van Basten. Or an opponent.

At the age of twenty-eight, I'd become a central midfielder. Sacchi had opened a new world to me. Between pressing and team play, I really started to see the fun in the game. It was no longer hard work. As often as not, we got angry when the match came to an end. We'd start yelling at the referee when he whistled the game over; we wanted to go on playing. We were A. C. Milan, "The Invincibles," we just didn't know it yet.

CHAPTER 10

Milan under Sacchi,
Just Like Bologna Under Maifredi!

If it's fair to say that there's always a new dawn, it's also true that beyond the rose-tinted sunrise you can usually glimpse a gathering storm. And not only a gathering storm, but a thundering tsunami. And, out of the center of the tsunami, there was always a team chairman, borne aloft by a chattering helicopter. And the clouds parted, and Berlusconi descended from the heavens (he—or, rather, He—will like that detail . . .).

In practical terms, though, the painting was actually the *Four Horsemen of the Apocalypse*: we were enjoying ourselves, but results were not forthcoming. That was the worst imaginable outcome for the man who was footing the bills. Himself, no less. He had a hard time landing on the field at Milanello, what with turbulence and air pockets. The weather reports seemed to point toward turmoil and change, especially after we were eliminated from the UEFA Cup by R. C. D. Espanyol, even though it was only the beginning of the season. Sinister clouds began to swirl around the Milan bench. What else is new? But, since He Himself had chosen Sacchi, and since Sacchi remained his favorite—his avatar here among us ordinary mortals—He kept his temper that time. He held it together very well. He believed deeply in his handpicked coach, and so He defended him tirelessly, especially against attacks from the sports press. The Communist sports press, I would have to imagine. There were a number of old-school journalists—Gianni Brera at the head of the pack—who questioned and criticized continually and relentlessly. Arrigo Sacchi was an innovator, and they failed to understand him. They had no patience with the things he tried to do. Sacchi was in the crosshairs, but he had a powerful shield of protection: Himself. He would often come to visit in training camp, He'd talk to us, ask us about work. He'd spend the whole day at Milanello, chatting with the whole team and then meeting with players for individual conversations, exploring our relationships with the coach. He conducted his first exit polls with us, and we already knew who had won: "Boys, I'm not getting rid of Sacchi." On that point, He had been clear from the very beginning, and he was right. We weren't winning, but in the locker room we all shared the same strong feeling: things were about to take a turn for the better. It was mathematically certain. Every week we knocked ourselves out, training hard, but, still, we were happy. Things couldn't go badly forever. Our style of play was carefully planned out; it would just take time for our movements as a team to become natural. That was the only problem.

In the past, He had been a reliable presence. But that was in the past. He was ultimately responsible for all decisions, and, before making those decisions, He consulted with the players. Often just with me and Franco Baresi. Once, in the spring of 1988, we were running into real problems as a team, on account of Claudio Borghi, the Chairman's latest infatuation—and, in reality, a complete waste of time as a player. He had discovered Borghi during the Intercontinental Cup of 1986; it was a bolt from the blue. He'd acquired him, but, since the two slots allowed by Italian law for foreign players were already occupied by Gullit and van Basten, He'd stationed Borghi on the Como team. Stay there, be good, and we'll be back to get you. At the end of the season, we were allowed to acquire another non-Italian player. And so He was pushing for Borghi, while Sacchi requested Frank Rijkaard.

Himself: "Arrigo, we're keeping Borghi."

Sacchi, with an expression of disgust on his face: "Mr. Chairman, taking for granted first of all that you are always right, that you are the greatest expert on soccer that the world has ever seen, that your choices are always spot on, as demonstrated by your decisions regarding coaches, it still may be that the player who could do the most good for the team is Rijkaard."

Himself: "But Arrigo, Borghi is Borghi."

Sacchi: "My point exactly."

So they came to a compromise: Borghi came to work with us at Milanello for the final training sessions of Sacchi's first season at A. C. Milan, as well as to play in a couple of exhibition games: one at home against Real Madrid and the other at Manchester against Manchester United. It was a double test, but we already knew, by his style of play, that he wasn't really in tune with the rest of the team. Just to make things more challenging, right before the A. C. Milan–Real Madrid match, Borghi injured his ankle, but insisted on playing all the same. He was clearly in pain on the field, but he managed to score a goal.

Himself: "You see Arrigo? He scored a goal."

Sacchi: "Yes, but aside from the goal, he didn't do a thing."

He was hobbling across the field, bent over in pain. He seemed like a soccer Lazarus, but with a substantial difference. He might have risen from the dead, but he couldn't seem to walk. It was hard to watch him. His ankle was swollen up like a cantaloupe, Manchester United vs. Milan was getting closer all the time, and Borghi refused to accept defeat. "I'm playing in this match." Sacchi: "I'm on your side, go ahead and play." We all understood that Sacchi wanted to send him out on the field, confident that Borghi would wind up with egg on his face.

So he started the game right by my side: he was charging forward, zigzagging as he went, a drunk in soccer shoes, but apparently fate was on his side. A pair of goals, both by Borghi: one, and then the other. Borghi-Borghi, *li mortacci sua*—damn his eyes. Playing at Manchester, against Manchester United. He smiled and said nothing: a bad sign. Sacchi neither spoke nor smiled: a very bad sign. At that point, we got involved. Sacchi frequently came to talk with us; he'd do his best to persuade us that Borghi had nothing in common with A. C. Milan, that he was a player out of place. "Coach, we couldn't agree with you more. That's exactly what we all think. We're on your side."

Then He Himself would call us, explaining that Borghi was the latter-day Maradona and that He Himself had discovered him: "Mr. Chairman, you are perfectly right. We think that you've got the inside track on this one. We're on your side."

We were hypocrites out of necessity, we all had families to feed and clothe. We were faithful allies of the guy that coached us, slightly less faithful allies of those who issued our paychecks. I never understood how Sacchi managed to get the boss to change his mind. There were certainly harsh verbal battles. The only thing I know is that in the end, He gave in. And Borghi was sold, and Rijkaard joined the team.

A. C. Milan, "The Invincibles," had also become A. C. Milan, "The Dutchmen." In quotes, with capital letters, as a sign of respect, because we were just too good. *Gullitrijkaardvanbasten*, as if they were one player, with a single tongue twister of a name; say it without stammering and you'll have discovered the secret of immortality. He Himself lit up with pleasure at the thought.

Without Rijkaard, and with Borghi killing time on loan to Calcio Como SRL, we had won the Scudetto in the meantime. Under Sacchi, we'd immediately become champions of Italy, on the first try. Our sensations had become reality; we were in gear, waving "so long!" to our rivals over our shoulders. Waving good-bye in particular to Maifredi's Bologna, our archenemies. No one knows it, but, in theory, that was supposed to be our model team. Our contemporaries, the team we aspired to become. Not Herrera's Inter but Maifredi's Bologna. Sacchi was like a broken record: "Now, *they* know how to play soccer."

We couldn't stand it anymore; he said the same thing, all day, every day, repeatedly, on the hour and half hour, in his inimitable accent: "*Ragassi*—boyz—you have to do your best to play like them. Maifredi's Bologna F. C. is the best team in soccer." At first, van Basten always had the same reaction: "Manfredo? Who is this Manfredo?" He was accustomed to Ajax, coached by Johan Cruyff. That Sacchi showed Baresi videotapes of Gianluca Signorini, so he could copy his movements, is an historical travesty; that he relentlessly and tirelessly talked to us about "Bologna di Manfredo" is, on the other hand, a sad and undeniable fact. He had managed to make us hate a team we had no reason on earth to hate. The team of the legendary Renato Villa and all the rest. He was jerking our chain. Until finally, one day, justice was done. On 26 December 1987, Sacchi arranged an exhibition match with Bologna, an away game. We poured onto the field, our eyes bloodshot with fury, and I was angrier than anyone else, because that was St. Stephen's Day, and there's an especially lavish banquet that I was being forced to miss. My dear Bologna and my dear Manfredo, I'm going to serve you a bowl of lentils and a plate of *bollito* to go with it. Before we left the locker room, we made it very clear to Sacchi exactly what was about to happen: "We'll show you who knows how to play soccer and who doesn't."

We pasted them, 5–0. We caned them mercilessly. Van Basten—the player who was most resistant to the playbook, because he loved to play by instinct—was injured, but on the way back home he turned strangely ironic: "Coach, maybe Sacchi's A. C. Milan is better than Maifredi's Bologna F. C." He was happy, even if he was wrong.

One exhibition game made us stronger, then Arrigo took care of the rest. Before he asked us to do something, he always explained why. There was a reason for everything. We implemented an all-encompassing pressing, and our opponents didn't know which way to turn. They couldn't understand a thing. They tried to play their game the way they were accustomed, and we suffocated them with our inescapable defense. In comparison with Roma, we were a very different group of players: we were less playful, we were a little more aloof.

The second match that changed our lives was the one we played against Napoli, at the Stadio San Paolo, in the last few weeks of the 1987–88 championship season. We were one point apart in the league, but we knew that there had been an earthquake in their locker room. Seismic tremors that made us confident of victory, in part because we had just won our derby—the *Derby della Madonnina* against Inter. Even before we ran out onto the field, we knew the game would end with us many points ahead, just as our opponents knew in advance that they were going to lose.

We were hurtling downhill through the championship, and at the bottom of the hill the Scudetto awaited us. Diego Maradona had issued clear orders: "When I play, I don't want to see a single black-and-red banner in the stadium." But we were there, and we were stronger than banners and fans. Napoli 2–A. C. Milan 3; we're the ones, we're the ones, we're the champions of Italy. We, and Him. Meanwhile, van Basten pestered a steward: "Excuse me, have you seen Manfredo, by any chance?"

CHAPTER 11

I Decide the Formation.

S acchi doctored the results of my athletic trials, especially my times on thirty-meter sprints. He didn't want me to know how bad they were; in his way, he was trying to boost my morale. Let's put it this way: in a race, a cement traffic post could probably beat me. Two-man sprint? I'd come in third—a distant third.

I was slow, but that's actually why we won the Italian championship. I couldn't perform any overlapping plays with Ruud Gullit; that was really the point. Ruud was a missile, I was a crawfish. A blowfish trying to keep up with a barracuda, which is physically impossible. And yet, in the early days, Sacchi believed in this formation, and he would insist on our playing in a 4-3-3 formation on the pitch. Four defenders, three midfielders—me on the right (with His approval), Bortolazzi in the middle, and Donadoni on the left—then three strikers, namely Virdis, van Basten, and Gullit, in front of me. There was one play that called for me to overlap with Gullit. If you don't know exactly what that means: if Ruud had possession of the ball, I was supposed to run at top speed up the field, cut behind his back, and receive his pass as quickly as possible. Once, twice, three times, a hundred times: the same thing always happened. Gullit would pass the ball to a phantom, because I just couldn't run fast enough. By the time I got there, the ball was already out of bounds. Sacchi would get irritated: "Come on, Carletto."

"Come on what? Dreadlocks here runs three times as fast as me. I couldn't keep up with him on my motorcycle."

We tried it forward, backward, and sideways, until Arrigo finally gave up: "Boys, let's try a 4-4-2 formation. With Ruud as striker and Carletto central midfielder." To put it simply, that was the formation that won us the Scudetto—the Italian championship. Just for starters. And it was all due to my two wooden legs.

People thought of that A. C. Milan as a remarkably talented team. Well, that's obviously not true; Roberto Colombo was one of our players . . . We had a good goalkeeper, Galli, but there were only three genuine thoroughbreds: Baresi, Gullit, and Donadoni, and all three of them were quite young. Maldini was still just a youngster, a phenomenon waiting to be discovered. What really made the difference for that team was our sense of being a group, and a strong sense of belonging, of loyalty. Loyalty to the team, to the owners, to our colors. Credit was due to the youth program, where many of the players had grown up. Galli, Costacurta, Baresi, Maldini, and Evani, lifelong Milan fans—footballers who had learned to walk at Milanello.

A. C. Milan, "The Invincibles," a homegrown team, with a defense that endured for many years. We could say that it still endures today. Tassotti-Baresi-Costacurta-Maldini—it could have been worse. It's a legend that is constantly evolving, handed down from year to year, from generation to generation, from symbol to symbol. Gattuso and Ambrosini will be the next lead tenors, if the mass hallucinations of the market will allow it.

Over the past twenty years, A. C. Milan has been consistently victorious because it has managed to preserve the same spirit it had at the beginning. With a deeply Italian core, another fundamental aspect of the team: players who lead the others, taking them to another level, with their behavior, discipline, and character. Foreigners included. There are always five or six Italians, and their presence is crucial; it is thanks to them that the tradition that Sacchi built continues. How long it will endure, I truly cannot say. Everything changes, everything always becomes more challenging. Over the past twenty years, the chairman has remained the same person, the managing director has remained the same person, the team manager has pretty much remained the same, in the sense that Silvano Ramaccioni was replaced only recently. There hasn't even been much turnover among the cooks and waiters at Milanello. It's always been a family business. The only significant change is that, because of his political obligations, Berlusconi has been less involved. His absence has been noted. He is rarely present at Milanello; during my last season, there were only occasional phone conversations about specific issues. From time to time, he'd call to ask how the players were doing, what formations I planned to field.

Note to the outside world: I decide on the formations—I alone, in all cases—and I want to make that point clear once and for all. Of course, Berlusconi has asked me more than once to explain why I excluded this player rather than that one, and we may even have argued in some cases when I chose to sideline one or another of his favorites, talented and skilled players that he has a hard time seeing cooling their heels on the bench. Lately, Ronaldinho; in the past, Rui Costa. He loved van Basten and Savicevic; he adores Kaká, even though he decided at a certain point to sell his contract.

If the chairman of your team asks you to explain the reasoning behind your decisions, you have an obligation to do so. It's a coach's duty to his employer. It makes sense. Berlusconi's general philosophy is well known; how many times have we heard it? "I want a team that is capable of winning championships in Italy, Europe, and around the world—a team that plays spectacular, exciting soccer. A team that embodies the principles of fair play, dedication, and discipline. A team that is master of the field and of the game."

This is just to say that the guidelines of today were already the guidelines back then. A team that can win, a team that plays exciting soccer. Sacchi was the first to succeed. Working with Sacchi, I also understood the importance of respecting a referee's decisions, even before Moggi and Giraudo explained it to me, with reference to De Santis. During the Milan–Empoli game at San Siro in 1988, I was given my third yellow card of the season, which meant one more and I'd be disqualified; the next game was scheduled to be played in Rome. Against my Roma. For the first time, I would be playing at the Stadio Olimpico as a former player. I didn't want to miss that opportunity, I couldn't get a fourth yellow card. I asked Silvano Ramaccioni to accompany me to the office of the referee, Rosario Lo Bello; I knew him because he'd come to see me when I was out of commission, along with Nicolini, an assistant to his father, Concetto Lo Bello. This guy Nicolini had a farm near my house where he raised veal calves. It was nice of them, I always appreciated it. So I went to Rosario Lo Bello, and I started talking immediately: "Signore Nicolini asked me to give you his regards," even though I hadn't seen him for months. "And I'm really hoping to play a good game today. The only thing that's worrying me is this: I'm on the brink of suspension, and on Sunday I really want to be playing against Roma. I really care about that, so I'll do my best to play right."

"Carletto, that's your problem."

I understood a number of things from his answer. Most importantly, that I had just fucked up. "Completely," Ramaccioni reassured me.

On the field, the score was 1–0, in our favor, with a goal by van Basten. In the last minute of play, we got a throw-in, I went over to the touchline and was about to throw and then changed my mind and handed the ball to Tassotti instead. Yellow card. Warning for delaying the restart of play. I was just wild with fury. After the match, I waited for Lo Bello in the tunnel, and I gave him several powerful pieces of my mind. Result: disqualified for two days, because, in his report, he also mentioned our pregame conversation. We appealed the decision, and got a one-day reduction, but I had to miss the Roma–Milan game nevertheless. That day's lesson: mind your own goddamned business. Especially when you get the unhealthy idea of going to visit the referee in his locker room. Especially when that referee turns out to be a traitor.

We first met Dieter Pauly at the Marakana Stadium in Belgrade, playing against Red Star in a UEFA Champions' Cup match the year after we won the Scudetto. I still detest Pauly today. I hate him, and I hate that animal Stojkovic. At the home game at the San Siro, we traded blows throughout the match; I gave him a couple of kicks and I'd been given a few warnings, but, as far as I was concerned, it ended there. Not for him; he waited for me in the tunnel to the locker rooms. In his native tongue, he said he'd be waiting for me when it was his team's home game. In my own native tongue, I told him that I couldn't wait for the chance, that I hoped those two weeks would go by in a hurry. He spoke in Austro-Hungarian, I answered in Emilian dialect; we understood one another perfectly. And, in fact, he was there, waiting for me in Belgrade, in a stadium with 120,000 spectators all baying for blood. There was a sense of tension, the atmosphere was strange, war was about to break out in the Balkans, and you could sense it. Everyone sensed it. Before Stojkovic walked out onto the field, he came to see me: "I'll see you out there."

"No problem, that's what I'm here for."

Four minutes into the game, I saw the ideal situation: he had the ball, I caught up with him, waited until the moment was right. I did my best to break his ankle, and I came pretty close to doing it. The referee, who was supervising his last Champions' Cup match, gave me a yellow card. Since I was already facing suspension, I was forbidden to play in the following match. Which, unfortunately, would be played against Red Star the following day. Around fifty minutes into the match, a tremendous blanket of fog descended on Belgrade, the Bogeyman suspended the game, and play was resumed twenty-four hours later. We won the rescheduled game on a penalty kick, after a regulation goal by van Basten that Pauly had failed to see. After all, he felt he had to earn his paycheck. And I had to give a meaning to mine, signed by a very angry Arrigo Sacchi: a fine of fifty million lire ($40,000). The most expensive yellow card of my life. To hell with Pauly, and to hell with Stojkovic.

Despite their best efforts, in the end we won the Champions' Cup (and the chairman revoked my fine). We won 4–0 against Steaua Bucurest, at the Nou Camp in Barcelona. In the semifinal we had eliminated Real Madrid, which Berlusconi had predicted in the locker rooms at the San Siro: "We're going to win with a *goleada*—a wave of goals." And, in fact, it was Milan 5–Real Madrid 0. He was already foretelling the future. He'd certainly seen the future in Sacchi, who gave him, in the years to come, a Scudetto, two Champions' Cups, two Intercontinental Cups, two European Super Cups, and an Italian Super Cup. Masters of Italy, Europe, and the world. The game was worth playing.

CHAPTER 12

A Double in the Last Match

C arletto, I'm leaving to coach the Italian National Team. I'd like you to come with me."

"Thanks, coach. I never thought of myself as a player who could still be national-team material."

No comment, just a deep sense of embarrassment instead. The season was coming to an end, and Sacchi was telling me, in deepest secrecy, that he was about to leave A. C. Milan. But he was also making it clear to me that my career as a footballer was coming to an end, because what he was really saying was: "Do you want to come along as my assistant coach?"

Arrigo Sacchi knew that his time at Milanello was ending (and when your time is up, the sooner you realize it, the better), and he was already preparing to set off on a new adventure: Italy. The national team. To combine his thousand tactics and formations into a single idea. He was the Garibaldi of Fusignano. Before that day, it had never occurred to me that I could become a coach. Arrigo's suggestion was a blinding revelation to me. For the first time, I saw myself on the bench, and, I have to say, I liked the idea. I immediately saw it as a major opportunity. It was 1991, I was thirty-two years old, I had wobbly knees, and I could continue as a player, but no one knew for how long.

Sacchi, with his great big sunglasses, twice the width of his face, left without a backward glance. For me it was more of an *arrivederci* than a good-bye.

So long, Arrigo Sacchi; hello, Fabio Capello. Not that I was all that happy to see him. His arrival marked the beginning, for me, of a period of ruthless competition, of being pushed aside, of feeling unwanted. The more I found myself on the bench, the more I felt like jumping over to the opposite shore, the one occupied by Sacchi, where you made decisions without having to run.

You won't like everyone you meet in life. Fabio Capello and I had—and have—different personalities. The problem—a problem I still encounter on the coach's side of the equation—is that it's very difficult to separate a professional relationship from a human relationship. If a player winds up on the bench or in the stands, by the very nature of things he can't feel a deep sympathy for his coach. The relationship doesn't take off; it's inevitable, and that's what happened to us.

Capello was the first coach who didn't think of me as an unquestioned regular fullback; there was a young man that the team saw as having a great deal of potential. They gave Demetrio

Albertini many more options than they gave me. When Rijkaard was injured, I started a number of matches in midfield up until November, but then I felt like I'd been caught in a game of Monopoly: from the pitch to the stands, without passing "Go." Or stopping at the bench. Four months sitting there as a thoughtful spectator—in the sense that if you're sitting there watching others play the game you want to play, you have a lot of time to think. In fact, that's where I made my decision, sitting on the folding seats of the stadiums of half of Italy: I'm out of here.

The first season without Sacchi was destined to be my last with A. C. Milan. At first, I had a hard time accepting that I was relegated to being an extra, playing the occasional cameo role, and then I understood. Capello was a very serious manager, he demanded discipline and understood intuitively how to shape his team to disrupt his opponents' play. He was a master at reading a match; that was his strongest skill. From that point of view, I had to tip my hat to him. But as a human being—well, that's another matter. He was a grouch, he didn't know how to talk to players, and, most importantly, he didn't like discussing technical matters with us. A dialectical exchange of views on strategy was alien to him, and so it never happened. Maybe that's why there were so many verbal clashes with the players. Maybe that's why one day Gullit hung him up on the wall in the Milanello locker room. Once again, I had to tip my hat, but the Italian for hat is "*cappello*," and Capello was dangling from a hat rack—it almost seemed predestined—dangling with his shoes just a few inches from the floor. (Before then, I'd only seen something of the sort in Rome, when Liedholm, by himself, had lifted Turone and Pruzzo off the ground by their necks during an argument.) Anyway, that's how it went that time in Milanello.

Capello, reading the newspaper: "Ruud, you said things here that weren't true. You're a liar."

Gullit, without reading the newspaper: "Now I'm going to set you straight."

Brawl. I'm pretty sure that a lot of the players were rooting for Gullit, but we all pitched in and separated them.

But to Capello's credit, after anything of the sort happened he just canceled it from his memory. As if nothing had happened. He started over from nothing. He pretended not to remember, for the good of the team. And for his own good. I have to say that there are times when I am just like him. As a coach, I have witnessed a great many arguments between players; it's routine. Usually, I just watch; I keep my distance. If the argument drags out, I intervene; otherwise, I wait for them to resolve it on their own. When Clarence Seedorf first joined A. C. Milan, he would pick fights with everyone. It was one quarrel after another with his teammates, especially during the first year. Clarence likes to talk a lot, and he likes to talk about soccer. At first, since he was a new player, this habit of talking freely wasn't particularly welcome. He was considered a know-it-all, an egotist—somebody who would always tell you how to do it better. Kaladze and Rui Costa couldn't stand him. Just days after he arrived in Milanello, Seedorf already wanted to tell Rui Costa how to take the field and how to play. No one wanted to acknowledge his leadership because he was a new recruit. Over time, though, things improved. Because, in reality, Clarence *is* a leader. He rallies the team in the locker room.

I was still a midfielder, but I was already thinking like a coach during that last year of my career as a player. This helped me a great deal psychologically: on the one hand, I knew that I was about to leave an enchanted world; on the other hand, my future was fully mapped out. During that season, I had the time to understand clearly what I wanted to do. The idea of becoming assistant coach to Sacchi was exciting. When Capello sent me up into the bleachers, in my mind I had an answer ready for him: "Fine, you coach A. C. Milan, I'm going to coach the Italian national team." Which might not have been exactly true, but I liked to believe it.

When I decided that would be my last championship season, I never gave it a second thought. Even though Capello tried to change my mind: "You can't quit. You have to stay. You have to play for another year." Sorry, can't help it. Sacchi needs me. And there was also the fact that, in the meantime, for his first game as head coach of the Italian national team, in Genoa against Norway, he summoned me—theoretically as a player, though in fact I spent my time helping him to train the midfielders. He wanted me to get a direct sense of what my future would be like; he wanted me to have a good idea of my next job.

My career as a soccer player was coming to an end, and I was clear-minded and relaxed. I knew one thing for sure: you need to quit when you feel it, not when other people tell you. Otherwise it's too late. And I ended my career on a wonderful, positive note, at the San Siro playing against Hellas Verona F. C. under Liedholm, my first teacher. Il Barone and Il Bimbo, on the same field for the last time. As opponents, but only in theory, because he and I had never been enemies. Really, we shared a single heart in two different bodies. We were joined together by our heartbeat and our passion. Two images reflected in a single mirror; only the periods of time that we occupied were different. That's why I believe that, deep down, he enjoyed my last performance. We were already champions of Italy, and, since I wanted to play, Capello sent me in twenty minutes from the end. The others seemed more excited than me. I scored a goal. Then I scored another. My first *doppietta*, or double—in the last game of my career. Well, better late than never. A long ball up the field, then a nice little dummy. As I ran back to the middle of the field, carrying the ball, I saw Baresi and just tossed out—more as a joke than anything else—"Franchino, I can't quit now."

"Cut the bullshit."

The captain's words are sacred. That whole stadium was mine—even Berlusconi, who declared at the end of the match: "We are going to offer another year's contract to Ancellotti." That's right—Ancellotti, with a double *l*. No sooner said than done: the proposed contract arrived, but I'd already made my decision. I'd had all the time I needed to work it through, and I was confident, certain that the time was right. I don't remember crying, probably because I had no reason to cry.

As a soccer player, I'd won everything I'd set out to win. As a man, I had two wonderful children, Katia and Davide. As a coach-to-be, all I needed to do was imitate my mentors: Liedholm and Sacchi, two completely opposite ways of thinking, and yet two stars in the same constellation—my constellation, because I'd had the good fortune to meet them both. One tranquil, the other tense. One Swedish, the other from Romagna. The first slept on trains, the second screamed and shouted in his sleep. Liedholm for the snow, and Sacchi for the beach. I had experienced two extremes, and each of them had taught me how to win. It would be enough to absorb a little here and a little there, with a tiny—teeny tiny— dab of Capello, and I'd have the time of my life. I wasn't worried, I was just curious. I was finishing my first life and starting my second, and I didn't even have time to rest. I was my own boss, chairmen aside. Moreover, if I ate an extra bowl or three of tortellini, no one would bust my ass over it. Goffredo Mameli, poet and author of the Italian national anthem, had become my new idol from one day to the next. "Let us join in a cohort / We are ready to die / Italy has called." Arrigo's Italy, the national team.

CHAPTER 13

World Cup Dreams

Paris. When I met Abramovich, I looked out over the city skyline and glimpsed London. When I was there with Sacchi, on the other hand, I saw trees and flowers, more than anything else. On the field, I was his assistant coach; off the field, I was a traveling salesman. One match after another, players to study and analyze, constantly traveling around Europe—I liked it all. I learned a lot; and in Paris I even brushed up on my Latin. Early one morning, we were in the lobby of a hotel (decidedly not the Hotel George V...), with time to kill before catching the plane late that afternoon. Arrigo was even crazier than usual: "Carletto, have you ever visited the Louvre?"

"No, is he in the hospital? I hadn't heard he was sick..."

I was trying to be funny, but he was determined to take me to a museum: "Come on, Carletto, let's go to the Louvre, let's go to the Louvre."

"That's fine with me, fine with me."

We hopped into a taxi, and, before I could even dream of seeing the *Mona Lisa*, we pulled up in front. It was closed, locked tight, no admittance. "Arrigo, you're not thinking of going to the airport this early?"

"No, Carletto, let's go for a walk." Unfortunately, right next to the Louvre is an enormous park. Trees and flowers, stretching off into the distance. "Look, Carletto, it's beautiful. Let's go take a stroll in the park." Me, him, Paris, strolling together in the park, the birdies singing. One thought humming through my brain: please don't let anyone see us.

"Carletto, this will only take a few minutes." Just a few minutes. Well, 240 minutes, to be exact. Four full hours. A botany lesson like no other. Apparently, Sacchi knows every tree and every flower on earth. He knew everything. "Carletto, this is *Crataegus monogyna*." Well, of course it is; I'd know it anywhere. Perhaps if he'd told me it was a hawthorn tree, it might have been easier to work up some enthusiasm. "Wonderful, Arrigo. Just wonderful." I really didn't give a hoot, but I was afraid to tell him that. He stopped every three feet, craning his neck and explaining in detail: "Incredible, Carletto, there's *Narcissus pseudonarcissus*."

Well, I guess it must have been incredible, because I didn't have the slightest idea what he was blabbering on about.

"It's a trumpet narcissus, Carletto."

Hold the presses. I missed seeing the *Mona Lisa*, and you're trying to show me a trumpet narcissus? Is that like a Black Narcissus? Questions started to form in my mind. Deep, searching questions. Questions like: Why does time drag along so slowly in this goddamned park?

"Oh, there's *Rhodothamnus chamaecistus* . . . and *Impatiens glandulifera*. . . . Now, let me tell you a thing or two about *Ligusticum mutellina*."

Thank you, Arrigo—thanks from the heart. I really wanted to know all about *Ligusticum mutellina*.

I. Was. Losing. My. Mind. It was like *The Scream*, by Edvard Munch, except with a slightly chubbier face. When we got to *Ficus benjamina*, I raised the white flag. I just gave up. Nothing personal against *Ficus benjamina*, but enough is enough. At the end of the fourth hour, I glanced at my watch: "Arrigo, *annamo*—let's go."

"Yes, Carletto, we'll miss our plane."

Long live Alitalia.

It was during that same period that I began to see Sacchi in a different light. I was still intimidated, but our relationship became a little warmer, a little more personal. There was a new intensity. I felt a genuine love for the man. In the professional sphere, he continued to demand the utmost of himself, but also of those who worked alongside him. For me, that was the best way to learn. I liked it. Pietro Carmignani and I were his assistants, his deputies: Carmignani sat next to him on the bench while I watched the match from the stands and prepared the match report. The terrible match report . . . It was a detailed report on everything that happened on the field. Nowadays, it's simple; everything's computerized. But back then it was grueling, maddening work. Maddening—in fact, people probably thought that I *was* mad, because I talked out loud while my assistant made notes of everything I said. Pass by Baggio, shot by Albertini, Mussi breaks free, Baggio makes a run, Baggio takes a shot. A steady stream of words, exactly like that, from beginning to end, without a pause. Anyone who was unlucky enough to have seats near us eventually moved away. We were intolerable, but we did it out of necessity. It's what Sacchi wanted.

And, all things considered, as long as we were doing the match reports for the Italian team, it really wasn't a problem. The real problems began at the 1994 World Cup, in the United States. It was my job to prepare statistics on our opponents, but here's the thing: often, it was just two or three days before a match when we found out who we'd be playing against. Once we did, I had to watch the videotapes of that team's last three matches and, while I watched, do the match reports. And I had to do it all in a single night. But I learned a lot from it: I learned to focus on details. That went on until the Italy–Nigeria game in the quarterfinals. The usual routine, me in the bleachers annoying my neighbors: pass from Oliseh, Oliseh has a shot, Amunike picks up the ball . . . In the sixtieth minute, with Nigeria leading, 1–0, I started to have the nagging thought: what's the best way to get back into Italy unobserved? How can we avoid a blizzard of overripe tomatoes at the airport? Maybe we can take a ferry from the island of Lampedusa. Or else, come south through Como. Whether to return from the north or the south—a difficult choice. I stopped doing the match report, but I hadn't counted on Roberto Baggio: two goals, one in extra time, and Italy was ahead. More important, I hadn't counted on Sacchi: "Carletto, where are my statistics?"

My first "team":
Back in primary school at Reggiolo. Twenty-three players and a female coach, the perfect squad. I'm the first on the left in the front row.

Me in middle school, around fourteen years of age.

The troublemakers are always in the front row, even during finals (I passed with 44 out of 100…).

Ancelotti in the army with two fellow soldiers (at Barletta, 1980). Italy called me, even before Saachi did.

In Parma in 1978 (top), and the winner after a championship match in Reggiolo (bottom). The Serie C national team in… our official company uniforms (center).

Talk about flying high…
In this case, over A. C. Lecco.

Turone, Benetti, Amenta, Conti, and me. With Baron Liedholm in the middle.

My knee has never been my best friend.

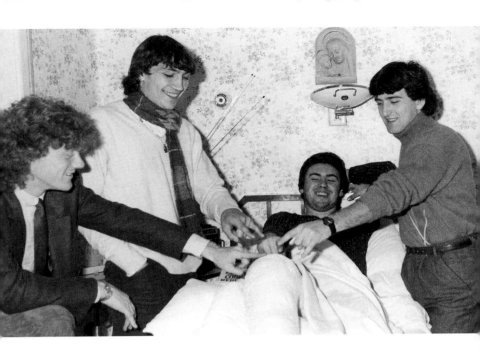

The exorcists Chierico, Bonetti, and Giovannelli try to cure me (top).

They weren't successful, judging by this picture (bottom).

Milan vs Avellino, November 1987: Ruud Gullit and me, when we were still young.

My goal against Real Madrid in the semifinal of the Champions League in 1989.

With Zidane, the best player I have ever coached.

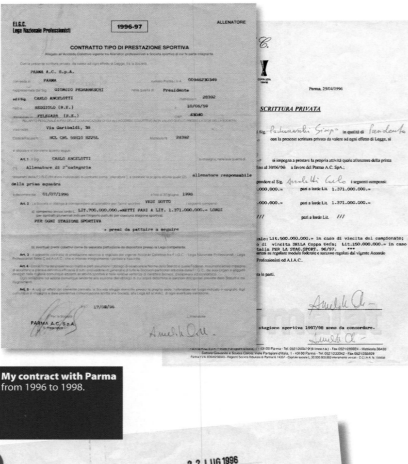

My contract with Parma
from 1996 to 1998.

The contract I signed with Juventus.
Nobody believed me at home…

Essere sereni, convinti della nostra forza, della nostra
idea e Concentrarsi per applicarla, lavoro sul
concetto della palla dietro di centrocampista _

- Fase difensiva, ho essere compatti, essere oli positive
va palla e ripetere.
- Fase offensiva, possesso veloce, ricerca della palla
dietro di centrocampista e attacco in profondità _
- Le

– Compatti, chiudici – determinati
– Entusiasmo, coraggio – semplicità
– Marcature fra ungeli e precisioni –

MARCATURE

CRESPO
DI BIAGIO
C. ZE
CANNAVARO
CORDOBA
MATERAZZI

MILAN – INTER 7.5.2003

FASE DIFENSIVA

- Squadra da tenea compatta, fare bene
le diagonali difensive, e di centrocampo.
- Attaccanti vicini alla squadra, lavorare per
evitare il lancio lungo dei difensori –
- Gilardino davanti alla difesa, pronto a
raddoppiare su attaccante, incunino, o
controllo posizione di Recoba –
- Difesa mobile, accompagnare il movimento
di Crespo in profondità, sulla palla libera,
salita se c'è occasione –
- Aggredire sulle fasce laterali, non dare spazi
per cross facile _
- Palla nostra metà campo, stretta sul centro,
dietro (di Baggio)
   – Marcatura a scalan su Recoba quando si stacca –

FASE OFFENSIVA –

- Fare un possesso efficace, senza fретта, non perdendo
palla, giocare a 2 tocchi, cercando di verticali non
dietro la linea dei loro c.c tutte le volte che è
possibile –
- Importante posizionarsi bene, Nesta, Seedorf e Brocchi
ai lati dei centrali.
- Scappare lo spazio sul movimento Seedorf e Brocchi.
- Inzaghi attaccare lo spazio in mezzo ai
centrali per allontanare la linea.
- Palla a Costacurta, Seva finta incontro e poi
dietro al terzino, con Brocchi o Seghiu.
- Cambiare il gioco per sfruttare il taglio degli
esterni.
- Non avere fretta, partecipare tutti alla costruzione
del gioco anche gli attaccanti; aspettare più attacco.

DIDA
COSTACURTA
NESTA
MALDINI
KALADZE
BROCCHI
GATTUSO
RUI COSTA
SEEDORF
INZAGHI
SHEVCHENKO

ABBIATI
SIMIC
ROQUES
REDONDO
SERGINHO
RIVALDO
TOMASSON

MARCATURE

COSTACURTA – DI BIAGIO
NESTA – CRESPO
MALDINI – MATERAZZI
KALADZE – COCO
INZAGHI – CORDOBA
SHEVCHENKO – CANNAVARO

RIGORISTI

PIRLO
RUI COSTA
SEEDORF
INZAGHI
COSTACURTA
SHEVCHENKO
NESTA
MALDINI
KALADZE
GATTUSO

SERGINHO
RIVALDO
BROCCHI
~~BROCCHI~~
TOMASSON
AMBROSINI
ROQUE J.

DA FARE

l'azione senza ~~possibilità~~

ABBIATI
COSTACURTA
NESTA
MALDINI
KALADZE
GATTUSO
PIRLO
SEEDORF
RUI COSTA
INZAGHI
SHEVCHENKO

FIORI
BROCCHI
ROQUE J
AMBROSINI
SERGINHO
RIVALDO
TOMASSON

INTER - MILAN 18.5.2003

FASE DIFENSIVA

- ~~Distacco~~ togli di presenza per lavorare sugli esterni.
- Rui pronto a uscire su Materazzi se porta palla, con contrоcompito e scalare in avanti
- Con palla laterale, Rui su Di Biagio, Pirlo su C.Silvo, evitiamo nostro ritorno a centroc.
- Difesa mobile, una in correzione, scappare in dietro un attimo prima.
- Pronti ad uscere in avanti se l'esterno riceve dietro, l'altro stringe verso il centro.
- Aggrediamoli con decisione e tempismo, quando siamo ben posizionati.

FASE OFFENSIVA

- ~~Rui~~ Sistematicamente guadagnare metri nel fraseggio con lo sprint dei terzini (RICEVERE PALLA IN AVANTI)
- Attacco gli spazi laterali dietro spalle del giocatore esterno o con i punti o con RUI o con un c.c.
- Se chiusi giocare su Pirlo che può verticalizzare
  sui passaggi e sostenere il gioco.
- Attacco a intera quando la palla è laterale oppure attacco la profondità quando la palla è centrale (TROVARE IL TEMPO GIUSTO)
- Quando l'attacco è centrale, attacco allargando, quando l'attacco è laterale, chiudersi la profondità dietro le spalle di Materazzi.
- Sfruttare eventualmente il 2 a 1 sulle fasce laterali.
- Essere sicuri, determinati, anche perché questa nostra frase. ~~Loro giocano~~ giocano la partita per evidenziare i loro limiti, con le nostre qualità.
  Questa partita vale e oltre il sigillo a tutto il nostro lavoro, ai nostri sacrifici, vogliamo che questo momento sia vissuto, dobbiamo essere cattivi.

With the President, Silvio Berlusconi (top).

Stefano Borgonovo with David Beckham (bottom).

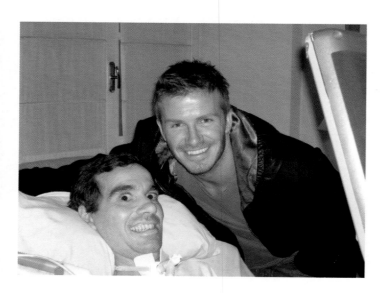

Champions of Europe. After beating Juventus at Old Trafford, at last, silver medals are a thing of the past. A pig can coach after all.

Everything flies higher in Athens... My last Champions League with Milan, in 2007.

Training with Didier Drogba, back at the San Siro for Chelsea's first leg against Inter in the Champions League in 2010.

Ray Wilkins and me at Chelsea's training grounds in Cobham.

The Chosen Ones.
With Sir Alex
Ferguson during a
game against
Manchester United
in the Premiership.

With Jose Mourinho
during the second
leg against Inter
in the Champions
League (opposite).

In training at Cobham before facing Atletico Madrid in the Champions League in 2009.

Eight goals and a trophy. Florent Malouda and I celebrate winning the Premiership title after beating Wigan Athletic 8-0 on May 9, 2010.

Me and Avram Grant, the manager of Portsmouth, during the FA Cup final on May 15, 2010.

We did the double.
Holding the FA Cup high after beating Portsmouth 1-0 to win two domestic trophies in my first season at Chelsea.

With Frank Lampard after winning the League a week before the FA Cup final.

Saluting the crowd with Chelsea's captain, John Terry, during the victory parade on May 16, 2010.

"Well, Arrigo, I only kept track until the sixtieth minute."

"Why, may I ask?"

He didn't understand. "Let's say that I had other things to think about."

And I wasn't alone in that dilemma. I saw plenty of sports reporters cursing as they bent over to pick up their notes from underneath their desks—notes they had crumpled into a ball and discarded just a few minutes earlier. More or less the same thing I had done. Videotape in the machine, hit play, and review the last thirty minutes of Italy–Nigeria.

I have wonderful memories of that 1994 World Cup, despite the weather. It was brutally hot, the humidity was intolerable, and after dinner all I felt like doing was going to bed and passing out. But every night after dinner, Sacchi would say, "Shall we go take a walk?" No, please, not The Walk, anything but The Walk . . . But there was no arguing; he always won, with only one saving grace, as far as I was concerned. There were no trees, there were no flowers. And no one spoke Latin.

We would walk out of the hotel—me, Arrigo, Carmignani, the fitness coach Vincenzo Pincolini, and the Federation psychologist Viganò—and with that little group on the loose in America, anything could happen. Four zombies shuffling along listlessly, and Arrigo, who never ran out of zip and vim. He'd only faltered once, the year before, when the Federation had sent us to New York for a preliminary inspection. In Brooklyn, the Italian-American families had organized a celebration, with two guests of honor: him and me. We were given a magnificent welcome, consisting of just three words: "Please invite Toto Schillaci."

And hello to you, too.

"He's our *paesano*."

That's when I whispered into Sacchi's ear: "Arrigo, let's get out of here while we still can."

But at the same time, they were screaming into his other ear: "Please invite Schillaci."

Thanks, we're crazy about you too. There's the Sicilian Mafia, the Calabrian 'Ndrangheta, the Neapolitan Camorra, and, let's see, from Puglia, the Sacra Corona Unita: the gang, as they say, was all there.

"Arrigo, listen to me, let's get out of here."

"Yes, Carletto, you're right. Let's go, let's go. It's getting uncomfortable."

"Quickly, Arrigo, before somebody fires a tommy gun."

Good evening to one and all, thanks for the kind invitation.

"Please invite Schillaci."

Oh, go fuck yourselves. Enough is enough.

I had fun in the States, too—intervals of fun between one game and another. Sacchi never stopped, he constantly talked about work, he never quit thinking about ways to improve the national team and the work he was doing. He taught me how to be a coach: how you plan the program, how you schedule the training sessions, how you manage different periods of time and different players. Working alongside him was one of the most interesting things that ever happened to me. I was only sorry about losing the final match of the World Cup, but really, I doubt we could have done much better. The heat and the humidity were overwhelming. We had made it to the end of the line, and the final match still lay ahead of us. The evening before the Italy–Brazil final, in Pasadena, we understood that we were done for from the conversation between Arrigo and the masseur, Claudio Bozzetti.

"Claudio, did you give the players their massages?"

"Yes, Arrigo."

"And how are their muscles?"

"Muscles, Arrigo?"

They were completely wiped out. Cooked. The players just managed to stay on their feet, out of inertia, or perhaps by some miracle. They had been playing matches in conditions of 100 percent humidity. During halftime, the players—Nicola Berti, especially—all came back to the locker room saying the same thing: "Substitute me. I'm not going back out there." They were red as lobsters. We'd put them in ice baths and try to get them back into shape. We played the first game, against the Republic of Ireland, in New York. We got to the stadium and went straight out onto the field. You couldn't survive for long. It was 108 degrees, 90 percent humidity. Those geniuses from FIFA had decided to schedule the game for noon. To encourage the players, Carmignani and I lay down on the grass and exclaimed: "How nice. At last, it's comfortable today. Cooler than usual, isn't it?" At that point, the players took a good hard look at us and decided that the sun had fried our brains. After the World Cup of 1994, I worked with Sacchi for another year, for the qualifying matches for the European Cup. Then Reggiana called me.

The American World Cup was fantastic—definitely more enjoyable than the two World Cups I experienced as a player, Mexico 1986 as a tourist and Italy 1990 without much excitement. In the United States, it was quite another thing—an endless thrill of happiness and joy. That's why I'd like to experience another World Cup, as the coach of an African national team (there's time for the Italian national team yet); that is, a team with nothing but potential—a team that remains to be discovered. A team that's not short of talent or quality, and maybe one with a big shot from the Ivory Coast. Me and Drogba—now there's a wonderful story in the making...

CHAPTER 14

Wobbly Benches

There are times when I stand up in front of a full-length mirror and act like a contortionist. I twist my neck and I stare at my ass. My fat butt cheeks aren't a particularly edifying spectacle, but that's not really the point. I look at them and I think: "There are so many wounds back there, even if you can't see them." One tremor after another, tearing through my skin. An earthquake, with an epicenter right there, sharp and violent, without a shock wave, and over time it's taught me a lesson: my ass is earthquake-proof. Sat on benches that have never stopped swaying and shaking, that ass has had to withstand every level of the Richter scale. Seismic shifts and jolts of voltage. A wave of irritation and annoyance that just won't stop: first an itch, then a pinch, and things went downhill from there. Everyone else is seated comfortably, and I'm perched on a volcano. Always have been.

I live with the threat of being fired. After I left Sacchi's Nazionale—the Italian national team—I became a real coach at A. C. Reggiana, in Serie B: after just three months, they were ready to fire me. There's always a first time. By the seventh week, we were in last place, three defeats and four draws; no one was doing worse than us. We were a ship of fools, and the captain was me. As if that wasn't enough, I was disqualified from Federation standing because I didn't have the proper certificate to coach a team. I found my assistant coach, Giorgio Ciaschini, while leafing through the pages of the *Almanacco Illustrato del Calcio*—the Illustrated Soccer Almanac. The fitness coach was a retired discus thrower, Cleante Zat. The team boasted the French player Di Costanzo, jocularly known as the poor man's Maradona. He recalled El Pibe de Oro in the way he took penalties; otherwise, he was definitely a poor man's player. I was in lovely company. I had even been jeered by my fellow townsfolk; it was more or less like being repudiated by your own family. I blame it all on the Reggiana–Cosenza game. We were winning 1–0; there were only nine men left on the Cosenza team after two sendings off. We kept jogging up to their goalposts in a vaguely festive, Christmasy fashion. We were so generous and good-hearted that we argued over whose turn it was to score; nothing like it had ever happened.

"Please, be my guest."

"No, my dear fellow, go ahead."

"I wouldn't dream of it. After all, today is your birthday; you should score."

Di Costanzo pipes up: "Can I score?"

His teammates, in chorus: "No, you only know how to take penalty kicks."

Just a few seconds before the end of the game, on the last play, their goalkeeper gave the ball a tremendous kick, and it flew all the way up the pitch into our area. Three players all leapt into the air at the same time: from our team, Gregucci and the goalkeeper Ballotta, who was already an old man, even back then, and, from their team, Cristiano Lucarelli, who was already a Communist, even back then. Two out of the three collided in midair: Ballotta and Gregucci. Lucarelli scored, kicking into an empty goal. The score was 1–1, and objections flew in every direction.

We went out for the eighth day of the championship after a week in training. I had two choices: either win or be sent home with a boot in the ass. This was the dancing bench (if it wasn't dancing, it was wobbling seriously), first edition. The decisive match was Reggiana–Venezia, and it was decisive for our opponents as well. There were lots of people who assumed: "Today is Ancelotti's last day." Wrong. Just fifteen minutes into the game, we were already winning, 3–0. They were not just wrong, they were dead wrong. By December, we were in first place, and by the end of the season, we'd been moved upstairs to Serie A. From jeering and catcalls to triumph: while waiting for the specialists, I had pulled off the first Italian miracle.

And we triumphed in spite of the terrifying January market. We were fielding the 4-4-2; the central midfielders, Mazzola and Colucci, seemed unreliable at first because they were still young. So we decided to intervene. We still needed to improve our strikers, and the general manager, Dal Cin, had reassured me: "We'll do great things together. It's a promise."

One day, right after the Anglo-Italian Cup, I walked into my little office. There, waiting for me, was Nando De Napoli, a former teammate on the Italian national team at the World Cup of 1986: "Nando, what a surprise! How are you?"

"Fine, Carletto. How are you?"

"Doing great, Nando. You should have called me. I didn't know you were in the neighborhood. If I'd known you were coming, we could have had lunch."

"Oh, yeah, well . . ."

"By the way, Nando, what brings you to this neck of the woods?"

"I'm your new midfielder."

I pretended to smile, but inside I was sobbing. I turned around, and standing behind me was Di Mauro, who was young, I guess, *once*, but that was years ago, when I was playing for Roma. I didn't ask him what he was doing there. I had a feeling I already knew. Another new player. Oh, thank you, Signore Dal Cin, you've really done wonders here. Both of them trained for a while, but I could see that it was hard on them, they couldn't keep up with the pace of Serie B. Both were at the end of their careers; both were recovering from injuries. One day, I decided to put them on the field, in an away match against Delio Rossi's Foggia, a team that didn't just run; it flew. They moved down the field a thousand miles an hour; we couldn't keep up with them even in our imaginations. De Napoli and Di Mauro were the pair of thinkers on the Reggiana team. Everyone knows that thinking takes time. Too much time, in some cases. While our reinforcements were clearing the rust out of their brains, the fanatics from Foggia were clearing us off the field, 3–0; it's been nice to know you. The next day, De Napoli came back to my locker room and practically went down on his knees: "Please, don't send me back out there. Those guys were crazy, they ran much too fast for me. I'm just a little old man."

Mazzola and Colucci suddenly became reliable; they were suddenly the right age, too. They started to play again, and they took the team all the way up to Serie A.

I have positive memories of that time. It was a happy time. It was the beginning of my career, but I expected that in my first year of coaching I would run into a lot more problems than I did. The players were fantastic. They helped me whenever they could, from the first day to the last. So did the team owners. It was a Reggiana with no famous names but with some exceptional people. Gregucci, Di Mauro, Ballotta, Mazzola, Simutenkov, Paci, La Spada, Di Costanzo, Pietranera, Gandini, Tangorra, Colucci, Schenardi, Tonetto, Cevoli, Caini, De Napoli, and Strada. Thanks, boys. In twelve months, I had already experienced everything: fear, whistles, catcalls, joy, the bottom and the top of the rankings, a near-firing, followed by a resurrection, a bad market, and even a poor man's Maradona. An incredibly rich experience. And a useful one, because, for the first time, I felt as if I should thank Capello, the gruff old guy who never let me play. In the meantime, he had also refused to accept the position of coach for Parma. He had come to an agreement with the team, but, at the last minute, he pulled out. With him gone, Parma called me. A team in Serie A. The Via Emilia—the Roman road that runs across northern Italy—is a sweet place for me: a return to my origins, to the city where I grew up as a player, where I'd played in the youth league. I was born in Reggiolo, but I lived in Felegara. So Parma was my second home.

I found myself in the middle of a transfer campaign that had been planned and executed by others (it's something that happens . . .). I was coaching players I didn't know, footballers that I'd never even heard of: Thuram, Crespo, Chiesa, Verón, Rivaldo, and Cafu. Then there was Bravo, coming from Paris Saint-Germain, Amaral, and Zé Maria (José Marcelo Ferreira). Well, I knew who Rivaldo was, but I didn't know the others. To make it worse, they wanted me to send a kid out to play goalie in Serie A, a child, a goalkeeper who was still green behind the ears. I thought they were joking, but they were dead serious. "Carletto, look; he's a good goalie. He can block anything."

"Fine, fine. What's his name?"

"Gianluigi Buffon."

"And who is he?"

The new team drafts were decided by Sogliano and Cavaliere Pedraneschi, the son of the Cavaliere Pedraneschi who, when I was just fifteen, came out to my small town to recruit me as a player for Parma after I had been rejected by Reggiana and Modena. I owed a debt of gratitude, through family connections, to the *cavaliere*, and he was just the first in a long series of mentors and benefactors. That is why I never objected to their recruits, which had in any case lost Verón at the last minute (who had been requested by Sampdoria in exchange for Chiesa), Rivaldo (who was asking for too much money and was replaced by Strada, whom I had coached when I was in Reggio), and Cafu (who decided at the last minute that he couldn't leave Palmeiras, a Brazilian club owned by Parmalat, the dairy company that also part-owned Parma).

"All right, I'll make do with what I've got in the clubhouse," which is to say, with Apolloni and Minotti, who were playing for the national team, Cannavaro, Bucci as goalie, and Zola. There was also Crippa—a tough player, for real.

The idea was to fight for the Scudetto, but we'd started out badly. I didn't know much. I could see Chiesa had enormous potential, but relations with Zola were becoming troublesome. I didn't want to abandon the 4-4-2 formation, so I tried moving Gianfranco to the left side of midfield, even if that wasn't his position. I hadn't yet guessed that the pair of Thuram and Cannavaro had limitless potential. I'd gotten a few things backward, which was absolutely my fault. Then Zola left, we sold Amaral, and we acquired Mario Stanic. So things were finally under control. At that point, this is what my Parma looked like: Buffon in goal; a four-man defense with Zé Maria, Thuram, Cannavaro, and Benarrivo; in midfield, from right to left, Stanic, Dino Baggio, Sensini, and Strada; Crespo and Chiesa as strikers. I still stand by it today. I was no visionary; back then, they were completely unknown. An incredible team, I know, but it's easy to say that now. In the first few months, we just couldn't work together; we were five teams from the bottom. Cavaliere (another knight of labor . . .) Tanzi got a new idea: "Let's get rid of Ancelotti." The usual earthquake, the usual lightning bolts, the usual burning sensation. In practical terms, I was the first man in history with stigmata on my ass.

CHAPTER 15

Ancelotti: Anti-Imagination

Maybe what Tanzi wanted was to take me to Parmalat. Print a nice SELL BY date on me, and sell me by the kilo—come to think of it, he would have made a good profit if he had. Carletto: best if consumed as soon as possible. Eat all you can.

Christmas was coming. The ultimatum came after a draw with Atalanta. There was only one condition: don't lose. Come to think of it, I wasn't sure not losing would be enough. Before the break, we had two away games, at Vicenza and at the San Siro, against Sacchi's A. C. Milan. The first match went well; Benarrivo saved me with a slicing shot from outside the penalty area. It was a lot more than just the goal of that Sunday; it was the goal of the entire week. The match ended 1–1; it could have gone worse, but according to Tanzi it had to go better. He didn't like us much in those days, but he couldn't cancel the Christmas dinner that he'd already planned at his house, just a few days before we left for Milan. We exchanged gifts; the players gave me a set of luggage. We were guests of someone who would gladly have skipped seeing us entirely. "*Buona sera*, Cavaliere."

"*Buona sera* to you. Do you know that our team is doing badly?"

Let's say I'd guessed it.

"Carletto, you should know that if you don't win against A. C. Milan, I'm going to fire you."

"Well, Merry Christmas to you, too, Cavaliere."

I lost my appetite, and it was the first and only time in my life, I think. Beat A. C. Milan in their own stadium. Impossible, or something like it. Word got around, and even Tanzi's closest advisers did their best to make him change his mind. "Mr. Chairman, we're playing at San Siro. Wouldn't a nice little draw be enough?"

"We have to win. And win we will."

Unless I'm much mistaken, I'd heard that phrase once before. By the end of the meal, he had begun to believe that a single point would save me. And he hadn't even had much to drink. Just a little two-percent Parmalat milk.

I had a bad feeling. I wasn't feeling optimistic. But I decided to take the initiative: the evening before the game, I asked the entire team to come to my room at the Hotel Doria. We opened champagne and we toasted: "To us." We said goodbye; we all agreed that it had been good working together. Short but intense. A farewell celebration—a sad occasion. Despite my sense of doom, the adventure continued. We won, 1–0. At San Siro. Against A. C. Milan. On the eve of the season's winter break. I always suspected that it was a sort of Christmas gift from Sacchi; maybe he thought that if I'd been fired it would have been a defeat for him too.

After the holidays, we won 1–0 against Juventus too. In that season, we won eleven times with scores of 1–0. Eleven times. Because we had an unknown goalkeeper, Buffon. Two central defenders who weren't anything special, Thuram and Cannavaro. An unimpressive striker, Crespo.

Another round, and the same gift. Just like in Reggio Emilia, in Parma we were turning the league on its head. From the bottom to the top, at the speed of sound. We let the Scudetto slip out of our hands in the return match against Milan, 1–1, but more importantly in Turin against Juventus. We were ahead once again by 1–0 when Collina called a scandalous penalty kick against us. It was shameful. There had been a disagreement between Cannavaro and Vieri, a scuffle between the two of them: no justification for a penalty kick. Invented. An optical illusion. While Collina was walking back toward midfield, I was yelling at him from the bench: "Nice work! Good job! Great decision!" I said it again: "Nice work! Good job! Great decision!" He turned and walked toward me; I stood up, he pulled out his red card. I couldn't believe it. "What are you doing?"

"I'm ejecting you."

That much I had already figured out; I was hoping for a more complete answer. Thrown out for my first offence; I doubt that many other coaches in history have enjoyed that particular honor.

After the game, I went to see him. I asked him why he'd ejected me. Chairmen of several teams hadn't been able to do it. What made him so smart?

"Well, I tossed you out because I read your lips. You called me an asshole."

"You're wrong; I thought it, but I never said it."

I guess he really was good; he'd read my mind. When things weren't going well, on the other hand, I tried to read my players' minds, asking for their help. When things were really on the line, just before we drew with Atalanta, I summoned the whole team to meet in the locker room. It was an emergency meeting; there were some things to straighten out. I was very direct: "Look, if things aren't working out between us, I think we might as well say it openly. If we can't get along, there's no point waiting for the chairman to fire me; if this meeting tells me that we don't see eye to eye, I'll go to Tanzi myself and tell him to find himself another coach. So please, let's talk in a spirit of sincerity." I have to admit, they were sincere. The first to speak sincerely was Alessandro Melli, who was open and honest: "I hope they fire you, so I can finally play some football." I appreciated it; we were there to tell one another what we thought. He did the right thing; he certainly helped me to understand the atmosphere in that group. In general, though, the team wanted to hold it together, to work together. They agreed with what I wanted to do. I had a strong feeling that things would improve quickly—and they did. We made it to second place, which meant we had qualified for the first round of the Champions League. Not bad for our first year.

The second year didn't go so well. We tried to reinforce the team, but we achieved just the opposite effect. We got to the first round of the Champions Cup, in the Stadio Ennio Tardini, against Borussia Dortmund, coached by Nevio Scala. That's where Crespo changed a city's opinion: he scored and then he clapped his hands over his ears; I think he was the first player to do it. "Oh, heavens. Has he gone deaf?"

I reassured everyone: "No, he's just pissed."

"Now jeer at me if you have the balls," he was suggesting—an unmistakable gesture.

Crespo wasn't well loved; he'd been jeered and whistled at frequently in his early times with the team. The fans didn't like him. He was talented, a serious young man, but they just didn't like him. Before that goal, it had been whistles, jeers, and cheers.

In the match against Borussia, everyone was asking me to replace him. Just after the match began, some guy right behind the bench started screaming: "Substitute. Substitute. Substitute." "Substitute, substitute, substitute." *Ma va' a cagher*—Oh, go take a crap. I kept him in, he scored a goal, we won, and I went to the press room: "I would like to inform the Parma audience that I will never pull a player off the field who is being jeered." Whistles and jeers, but I wouldn't substitute myself either.

During my time in Parma I came in for a lot of criticism, especially in my second and last year. Everyone had an opinion, and they sort of tended to look down on me. Parma (like Reggio Emilia) was historically a farming town, then over time it became an industrial capital, losing the peasant culture that I love best. We lost a match against Fiorentina under Malesani; so Tanzi, in hopes of victory, hired none other than Malesani as next year's coach. But without the Fiorentina team, which would have been a little too spendy.

I wasn't popular with the old executives of Parma either, especially because I'd decided against signing Roberto Baggio; they never forgave me. At the end of my first season with Parma, Roberto had already come to an agreement with the club, but he wanted a regular starting position, and he even wanted to play behind the strikers, in a role that didn't exist in 4-4-2. I wasn't willing to change my formation, and I told him so. I had just gotten the team into the Champions League, and I had no intention of changing my system of play just then. I called him up: "I'd be delighted to have you on the team, but you should know that I have no plans for fielding you regularly. You'd be competing against Crespo and Chiesa." I'd been rigid; I wasn't looking for conflicts or problems. He disagreed; I could already imagine his ponytail rising in protest. His answer was crystal clear: "I want continuity, I need to play all the time." And, in fact, from A. C. Milan he went to Bologna.

Now, years later, I regret how it went. I was wrong to be intransigent. Over time, I learned that there is always a way of allowing a lot of great and talented players to work together and get along. At Parma, I still thought that 4-4-2 was the ideal formation in all cases, but that's not true. If I had a time machine, I'd go back and of course I'd take Baggio. I could have handled the situation very differently. All of this, of course, caused problems for me. I was branded a coach who was opposed to attacking midfielders, and that wasn't entirely unfair. For that matter, the year before, I'd turned down Zola as well. Ancelotti, the anti-imagination. Give me anything, but not another number 10. The truth is that I was afraid of moving into territory that I thought I knew too little about. It was a lack of courage, but I made up for it in the years that followed. I found a new source of courage, in part because I went to coach Juventus. And I really couldn't bench Zidane.

CHAPTER 16

Montero and the Avvocato,
Both Crazy About Zizou

It felt more like a court of law than the locker room of Juventus F. C. The place was teeming with lawyers, all eager to defend Zidane; this is my first memory of the *biancineri*. When I think back to Turin, Zidane comes to mind. The Dream Player was presumed innocent, no matter what, and that presumption was defended ferociously by his incredibly expensive team of lawyers: Gianni Agnelli and Paolo Montero. Agnelli was the Avvocato, full stop— Italy's national "Lawyer"—while Montero was a lawyer without a law degree, but ready to take on all comers. An odd couple. United in the name of Zizou, a fiery comet that fell to earth from the starry sky, a poster that stepped down from the wall. Welcome to the world of mortals, Our Lord of the Soccer Ball.

They were his shadows, they were his guardian angels, they

never left his side. Agnelli was crazy about him; Montero was just plain crazy. When they looked at Zidane, they saw a pure and glowing light, a traffic light that was permanently green. A right of way to extraordinary transport, and he was certainly extraordinary; too bad for us if he often showed up late.

One day, during my first year on the Juventus bench (a year that began in February 1999), we were scheduled to leave for an away game, and Zidane hadn't arrived yet. He'd vanished, and his cell phone was turned off. I waited for a while, then I made a decision: "Let's go."

"But, Carletto, how will he catch up with us?"

"That's his problem."

From the back of the team bus, Montero jumped to his feet, marching up the aisle toward me. "Coach, we need to talk."

"Sure, Paolo. Let's get this bus on the road, and then I'm all ears." He marched up to the driver and crossed his arms. "No, that's exactly what we need to talk about. No one is leaving here without Zidane."

I took a few seconds to think it over. I evaluated the situation with a certain mental clarity: "Okay, here I am, facing a homicidal maniac who is staring furiously into my eyes as he clenches and unclenches his fists. Given the choice between the good and the not-so-good, he has always sacrificed the good: he aims at the ball, and he kicks your leg; he aims at your foot, and he kicks your leg; in fact, when he aims at your leg, he kicks your leg."

"OK, Paolo, let's just wait for him." The important thing, after all, is your health, right?

Zizou showed up ten minutes later, apologized for being late, and the bus pulled out.

Zidane was the greatest soccer player I ever coached—the sole inhabitant of a very different planet. Before every match, the Avvocato came into the locker room, said hello to Alessandro Del Piero, and then went straight to Zizou. He was head over heels in love; he took Zizou aside and had a little chat. It was a scene that I witnessed dozens of times. Often, Agnelli was accompanied by his grandsons John and Lapo Elkann; they would appear, greet the team, and go talk to Zidane. They were just like their grandfather. Then it was Moggi's turn: where's Zidane? And Giraudo: where's Zidane? And then Bettega: discreetly, in a private corner of the locker room, because he was shy.

That was when I started to get a little lonely. Everyone was ignoring me; they all came to see Zidane. Sometimes even the fans ignored me. For instance, one morning at Turin's Caselle Airport. We were returning from Athens, we'd just played an embarrassing Champions League match against Panathinaikos, and there, waiting for us as we got off the airplane, was a small mob of young men who weren't especially interested in paying tribute to our athletic prowess. As Zidane went past, they shoved him. That marked them for—well, maybe not for death, but sudden and certain punishment. Montero witnessed the scene from a distance, removed his glasses and, with an elegant gesture that struck me as incongruous, slipped them into a case. It was handsomely done, but it boded badly for the young men. A few seconds later, he was running at top speed toward the little cluster of hoodlums, fists flying.

Backing him up was Daniel Fonseca, another willing brawler. In my mind, I imagined a boxing announcer right behind them, hovering just outside the ring: "And that's a right, a left hook, another left hook. Technical knockout, that's a TKO. Zinédine is safe. I repeat, Zinédine is safe."

Oh, the beating those poor guys took. They left a few on the ground. The problem was that a few hours later, we realized they were soccer hooligans, and vicious ones at that. In fact, they came to pay a call on us in the days that followed.

Ours was a team that was always ready for a battle. A single spark was enough to unleash an inferno. Paolo Montero, Daniel Fonseca, Edgar Davids: the Ivy League, present and correct. If they caught a whiff of a brawl, they would rush in without thinking twice. One time, at the Stadio Olimpico in Rome during halftime, the whole team was already down in the locker room. We heard angry voices outside, the sounds of an incipient brawl. Montero shouted, "Where's Zidane?" (he really was sort of fixated ...) and bolted out in person to see what was happening. He rushed into the fray, only to discover that it was just a crowd of Roma players, angrily quarreling amongst themselves. They looked up to see a furious Montero bearing down on them, ready to mow them to the ground, for absolutely no good reason. Paolo Montero adored Zizou, and, for that matter, I adored Paolo, who was pure of heart and stout of spirit. He could easily have been a convicted felon, but he had a code of honor all his own. And a mission, for which he was willing to fight: "Keep your hands off Zidane."

Zizou's son, Enzo, was just as amazing as his dad. He'd come to the stadium and imitate his father's fakes. He never missed a move. He was a genius and the spitting image of his dad. I am increasingly certain that I coached a supernatural being: supernatural in every way, in his remarkable talent and in his great humility. Zidane is the soccer player who, in my life, produced the greatest array of chills, thrills, and sheer enjoyment—a living spectacle who put on an amazing show every single day. The best description of him that I ever heard came from José Altafini: "The way he used his foot, it was as if he were spreading butter on a slice of bread." He had one shortcoming: he never scored all that many goals, he didn't spend a lot of time in the penalty area. He seemed to be allergic to that section of the field, but he was an absolute master of all the others. Training was a thing he loved—a thing we all loved. He invented, and we watched openmouthed. I watched because that was my job; his fellow players watched because you can't stop an artist. You just admire his work.

Edgar Davids was one of the first players I talked to in my capacity as coach of Juventus. I liked him a lot, and I told him so immediately: "I like the way you play, your aggression, your determination, your decisiveness. It's clear that you never yield the initiative, that you're a fighter, a battler." I went on to catalog his physical endowments, his skills, and his natural gifts. He just stared at me and never said a word. More than stare, he glared at me, like I was a turd he'd accidentally stepped on. He listened, closemouthed. Finally, when I stopped talking, he enunciated a concept: "You know, I can play soccer, too." True, though technique was never his strong suit. He loved to work hard, but he hated to run, so every day I had to invent specific new training exercises with the ball. It was like giving medicine to a child: if you just give him a spoonful, he'll spit it out. If you hide it in a spoonful of Nutella, the odds are better. Before you could get Edgar to do something, you had to explain the reason why—which advantages and benefits it would bring to him. He was a perfectionist, and even a bit of a pain in the ass.

Alessandro Del Piero was less than happy when I first met him. When I got to Turin, he was trying to return to active play after the injury to his knee. He'd lost speed and reflexes, but I never lost confidence in him; he wasn't an amazingly productive player, but he was, and remains, invaluable. I could never do without him. I always thought that, even a few years later, when Capello was training Juventus but largely overlooking the team's captain. Ale, to use his nickname, is a born leader, and you can never overlook him. That's all I have to say on that matter. That first year, I had him play when he was in conditions that would have convinced another coach to bench him (Capello, for instance, would have put him in the stands, or else sent him home, suspended, without dessert). I felt that I had to help him; he deserved it. From a professional point of view, he has always been serious and determined. In human terms, he is a rare and priceless individual. In terms of technique, he's a thoroughbred. He has an essence that is hard to pin down, difficult to define in its beauty.

When I became head coach of Milan, I wanted to take him with me, and I even made a few tentative efforts to do so. But Del Piero is Juventus, and Juventus wasn't for sale. The Avvocato used to call him Godot, because everyone always waited for him but he never got there. Ale hated that joke. It made him angry, but he couldn't say so, because Gianni Agnelli was . . . Gianni Agnelli—an icon with an idea that was beginning to buzz around in his head. He wanted to bring Paolo Maldini over to Juventus. It was one of the rare occasions in which the Avvocato allowed himself to be swept away, putting a defender ahead of the rarer magic of the striker. Usually he was enchanted by goal-making artists. He wasn't alone in that tendency. A short while later, I would become acquainted with a chairman who—if he could have had his way, excuse me, His way—would have fielded eleven strikers, with the proviso that he could always fire me if he thought the team was unbalanced.

The Avvocato's dream—in that case, at least—never came true. Maybe that was why it was such a sweet dream for him. Maybe the times when he felt a yearning for Maldini were when he got in his car and had his driver head over to see us on the field. Or, I should say, to see him—Zidane. His perfect consolation prize.

CHAPTER 17

If You're Looking for Feelings,
Please Apply Elsewhere

As a pig that couldn't coach, I never really liked Turin. It was too gloomy, a couple of galaxies away from my way of life. Back off, posh guys—here comes the fat boy with a bowlful of Emilian tortellini. Juventus was a team I'd never really loved. In fact, it's a team I'll probably never love, in part because of the welcome that some higher intelligence reserves for me every time I come back there. It's always been a rival team; even when I was a little boy, I was an Inter fan right down to the marrow of my bones (hmmm, makes me think of beef broth), and completely obsessed with Sandro Mazzola.

Suddenly, I found myself on the other side of the barricade—in a sense, on the other side of myself. As a result of a purely professional decision. Unfortunately, I have always had a serious defect:

when I coach a team, I become its number one fan. It doesn't happen to everyone; I'm willing to bet money on that. But I always get drawn in emotionally. I am overcome with an all-consuming passion, a momentary crush. It's not that I'm a company man; I'm just an old-fashioned romantic. I respect the culture and the history of the clubs I work for. I think that's the right way to approach my work. A person ought to do it; a person has an obligation to do it. You can't just show up at a club one day and start issuing orders.

At Juventus, orders were issued by the Triad, and they always took good care of me. They took very good care of me. True, they fired me after just two and a half years, but that's another matter. As long as I was their coach, Moggi, Giraudo, and Bettega made me feel like I was the best coach in the world. With their words and with their actions. Their behavior was impeccable, as far as I was concerned.

I find it inconceivable for a club to question a coach's actions during the season. It's a baffling, counterproductive way to work. When I was with Juve, I knew that I enjoyed the respect of the top management, even when things weren't going well. There were harsh meetings, I saw more than one player on the verge of tears, but even at times like that they treated me like a king. They were always there, at training and during matches; they lived with the team, they knew everything about everyone. Absentee executives aren't helpful, and they understood that.

Juventus was a completely new environment for me. Very different. I never really felt comfortable. I was a cog in the machine— just another employee in a huge corporation. If you're looking for feelings, please apply elsewhere. On the job, everything went smoothly, but outside the workplace, nothing. I saw Moggi every day, we were neighbors. I lived downstairs from him, on the Via Carlo Alberto. Of the three members of the Triad, I was closest to him. He liked me, he cared about me, and the feeling was mutual. I still talk to him occasionally; the same goes for Giraudo. But Bettega basically vanished into thin air.

That Moggi—Lucianone, as he was known—was an important and influential person was common knowledge. Even a few referees seemed to be aware of it. One in particular. Everyone respected Moggi, and so, in effect, there could be a sense of intimidation at times. His strength, and later his downfall, was his public relations: he never said no; he would meet with as many as thirty people a day. He was outgoing and open-minded, which made him more powerful and more widely hated. The fact that he was with Juventus made him powerful, and that is why there were people who found him intimidating. They were all so many little lambs bleating in the presence of a ravening ogre, who wasn't really an ogre after all. Neither an ogre nor a saint, no question about it.

Gathered around him, Luciano had lots of little helpless lambs but not many Johnny Lambs, to use the nickname of Gianni Agnelli and his family. No, it was members of the Agnelli family that Luciano lacked. The important decisions all fell to Umberto Agnelli, the Dottore (the Doctor), who was more genuine than the Avvocato. The Agnelli I liked best was Umberto's son Andrea, a person of great moral substance. A remarkable young man. He encouraged me, he helped out when he could, he told me not to worry when the victories weren't coming in as we'd hoped. He was a point of reference.

The family man, in particular, was Giraudo, though he too was capable of laughing and playing pranks. Once, we made a bet on the outcome of a match; I accepted the bet, even though he—how to put this—had a certain advantage. He often predicted the results of others . . . What was at stake? Oh, just dinner in a restaurant for twenty. I lost the bet, of course. Giraudo decided to exaggerate: "Carletto, we're all going to a place that specializes in truffles." Truffles? Affordable! The Piedmont Vacation Group, as we called ourselves, went on the road, from Turin to Castello di Annone, near Alba, the home of the white truffle. Among the starving masses we brought with us was Galliani, who at the time was a very, very close friend of the Triad. Add in Galliani, and it goes from a Triad to Four of a Kind. From poker to porker: None of them seemed to have eaten anytime in the past few months. They just kept grating truffle after truffle. They were eating truffles like they were popcorn. It never seemed to end. Instead of scratch and win, it was grate . . . and let Carletto pay. And that's not even to mention the rivers of champagne, "the best champagne in the house," as I seem to remember Giraudo telling the waiter—more than once. Everyone was sloshed on champagne: finally, a bubbly, cheerful Juventus. And while they were eating and drinking, I was calculating the check in my mind, trying to figure out how much I had lost on that (probably fixed) bet. At least two hundred thousand lire apiece, which, multiplied by twenty, added up to four million lire. That, it turned out, was optimistic: "Signore Ancelotti, here is the check." Ten million lire. Ten. Million. Lire. I expected a receipt, but what they brought me was an ancient Greek scroll. A foot and a half of bill. I felt faint; I pulled out my checkbook, hating all twenty of my guests as I did so. Galliani's tie had veered from purple to yellow, he'd guzzled so much champagne. Behind my back, I heard someone laughing. It was Giraudo. He could be likable, even though in public he was always serious, at times verging on arrogant.

"It was a joke, Carletto. I'll pay." The future of my daughter and son, Katia and Davide, suddenly brightened. Their inheritance was safe.

Giraudo and Moggi always made me the butt of their pranks. One day in Athens, in November 2000, they made me look like a dickhead, long before the Chosen One uttered the immortal phrase at Appiano Gentile: "I am not a dickhead." We were in training, and one afternoon I dared to take a nap. The phone rang; by some miracle, I managed to locate the receiver, and I answered: "Hello?" "Wake up, Carlo, there's a call for you from the Avvocato." I stood up, snapping to attention, a rumpled, befuddled figure, and tried to regain my grip on reality. Over the phone came the refined accent of Gianni Agnelli, with his mushy pronunciation of the *l*'s and *r*'s in every word, including my name.

"Hewwo, Cawwo, I just saw a fantastic pwayer from the Ivowy Coast."

Hold everything—stop the presses. Let me spell this out: the Ivory Coast. There is no national team on earth that I love more than the Ivory Coast, after the Italian team.

"He is a phenomenon, his name is Kabungaguti. You've seen him pway, I pwesume?"

The world famous Kabungaguti: who the hell is he talking about?

"Avvocato, sir, I actually don't know anything about him, but I can find out. I'll request videotapes right away."

"He's a gweat champion, I'm supwised at you, Cawwo. How on earth could you not know about Kabungaguti?"

I felt like an ass. I was tempted to put on a hat with donkey ears and wear it to the coaches' technical meeting. I got dressed and went down to the lobby. I saw Moggi and hurried over to him: "Luciano, the Avvocato just called me."

"Really? What did he want?"

"He asked me about a player from the Ivory Coast, some guy named Kabungaguti. Have you ever heard of him?"

"Have I ever heard of Kabungaguti? What a question. Everyone's heard of Kabungaguti."

"Everyone but me, apparently."

"Well, you'd better study your players, Carletto; we've practically drafted him."

Just then, I heard a familiar voice. His voice, the voice of the Avvocato, Gianni Agnelli: "But Cawwo, how can you not know about the gweat Kabungaguti?" At that moment, I thought only one thing: "I'm screwed, he's going to send me away to coach Torino." I turned around to grovel and apologize, and there stood Augusto Bellani, travel agent and tour organizer for the Agnelli family, almost paralytic with laughter. He couldn't stop laughing. I had never heard about one of his greatest talents: he was the finest living imitator of Gianni Agnelli. He could, of course, only imitate Agnelli's voice: physically, they only ever made one Gianni Agnelli. To tell the truth, I never really knew whether the Avvocato loved the Triad. He was a man who lived on sensations, thrills, and love affairs. Love affairs with everything that was beautiful, everything that pleased him. Incredibly wealthy and yet, at the same time, fond of the simple things in life—aside from Zidane. He never really connected with Moggi and Giraudo—maybe with Bettega.

One day, toward the end of my period in Turin, Agnelli asked to meet with me alone. He gave me an hour of his time, a conversation in which he expressed affection and confidence. "We didn't win the championship, but we had a good season. You're a good person, Carlo. And remember, that's what matters most in life."

Sure. And, in fact, the next day I was fired.

CHAPTER 18

The End of a Story that Never Began

One hundred and forty-four. That's one-four-four. It's like the old emergency hotline number of the last century—144. "Give us a call, Juventus fans. My name is Carletto, and, pig though I may be, I'll make your wildest fantasies come true. All but one: winning the Scudetto."

During my time as coach of Juventus, we scored 144 points in two seasons, and twice I took the team to second place. Other teams became champions of Italy, though. First Lazio, then in the second year, Roma. In that period, the Italian capital came alive. If you would like the universal deluge unleashed upon Perugia, please press one; if you prefer a goal by Nakata, press two; if you wish to speak with a (smooth) operator, call Moggi on a Swiss cell phone. The one thing you can be sure of is that he will always answer.

We were beaten the first time by a rainstorm; the second time, the following season, by a goal put in by a Japanese player who technically wouldn't even have been allowed to play if it weren't for the fact that they managed at the last minute to get rid of the rules on players from outside the European Community.

Without delay, Juventus decided to get rid of me. They made the decision, but no one had the courage to inform me. No one but the sports journalists in Turin, who seemed to have known all about it in advance: "Carletto, you know that, after this season, they're going to fire you, don't you? They've already cut a deal with Lippi."

"Stop pulling my leg."

"We're totally serious; you're a dead man walking."

Take that. I've always had excellent relations with Turinese sports reporters. Maybe the fact that almost none of them were Juventus fans helped.

"Boys, you've lost your minds. I have a contract in my office."

"Take another look at it. Maybe it's a cell phone contract. Maybe Moggi named you responsible for the bills for his seven cell phones...."

Everyone was ready for their television appearance. I've certainly heard of coaches fired through the press—lots of them— but I've never heard of a coach fired by the mass media themselves. And that's what was happening to me.

I couldn't believe it; my contract had just been renewed—at the end of a ferocious battle, not a negotiation. As soon as we were eliminated from the Champions League, in December 2000, I was summoned to club headquarters. Moggi, Giraudo, and Bettega on one side of the table, and me on the other side. Three against one—

not sportsmanlike. It was obvious they were going to win. They began the meeting with: "We've been eliminated from the finals, but we don't care about that. You're doing a wonderful job, so we want you to stay on with us. In your contract, there's an option for a renewal; we'd like to exercise it. How much do you want?"

"Two and a half billion lire, thank you."

The least I expected was a "you're welcome." But that's not what I got. Since they did everything at the same time, like a synchronized swimming team, they all stood up brusquely—all three at the same moment—turned on their heels, and left the room. Every movement was perfect, not a second's hesitation, perfect coordination. I wonder if they practiced that little exercise. First the right leg, then the left leg, torso erect, head turned toward me, ferocious expression, about-face, hup-two, three, four, parade-step toward the door. Moggi swung the door open, Giraudo and Bettega moved their arms like Moggi, as if they were going to open the door too, and then . . . they were gone, slamming the door behind them. Oh, lovely routine; I'd give that a solid ten. Perfectly synchronized. That wasn't the Triad, those were three little mermaids at the Olympics. And me? An asshole, sitting there all alone in the meeting room. Twenty minutes later, Moggi stuck his head in the door: "What are you still doing here?"

"Could we agree on two billion lire? . . ."

"Beat it."

"How about 1.7 billion?"

"Get the hell out of here!"

Beginning the following day, our discussions moved to the pages of the newspapers, in the sense that they would issue statements and I would read what they had to say—including the statements of Umberto Agnelli: "Here we seem to be dealing with someone who's gotten a swollen head." That wasn't exactly fair. My head was oversize, no question, but it had been since birth. Anyway, we came to an understanding after another couple of meetings. Me and the black-and-white synchronized swimming mermaids.

Still, I couldn't relax. It was all the fault of my friends the sports journalists; they kept pestering me about it: "You're out, Carletto, resign yourself to it. They made a deal with Lippi back in December."

I heard them say it so many times that, just before the time came to put my signature on the renewal, I decided to put in a call to Milan's team manager, Ariedo Braida: "Listen, I'm about to complete negotiations for a renewal of my contract. If there are any opportunities for me to come coach for you next year, I'll wait." I wanted to send a signal, create an alternative for myself. But I'd only created an alternative universe in my head, because Braida started to stammer and hesitate: "Well, Carletto, see... you understand... how can I put this... I'm not sure we can go against Juventus." And in fact, they couldn't: the two teams were practically a single entity. Mil-entus. Or Juv-ilan. "We can't take away their coach; it would be crossing a line."

Moreover, Braida had left out a few details; he'd already hired Fatih Terim, aka *Imparator*, but he couldn't tell me that yet.

Before long, the Triad would torpedo me. One morning, after the Juventus–Roma match, which ended with a 2–2 draw—the match with Nakata's goal, the match of the reversal from a 2–0 lead, the match where Edwin van der Sar showed off the team specialty, penalties *ad ballseam*—I received a phone call from Umberto Agnelli's office: "Come to Fiat headquarters, please. It's urgent. The Dottore wants to speak to you."

Since I didn't know all that much about manufacturing automobiles, I had a funny feeling I already knew what the topic of conversation was likely to be. To make sure, I called Moggi.

"Ahò, Carletto, e che vuoi?" he greeted me on the phone: Carletto, what do you want now?

"Listen, Luciano, the Dottore called me on the phone. He wants to see me. Do you have any idea what he wants?"

Click. Boom. He slammed the phone down in its cradle. Just as I thought: he wants to fire me.

I showed up for the appointment. Umberto Agnelli didn't waste words: "My dear Ancelotti, the new Juventus coach is Marcello Lippi."

You don't say. Who'd have thought it? My last game with Juventus was in Turin, against Atalanta. At the end of the match, I entered the press room and the journalists—the ones who knew what was going to happen long before I figured it out—burst into a lengthy applause. I'm sort of ashamed to admit it, but that moment moved me deeply. Like a child. Because I understood that they loved me and that—aw, shucks—I loved them. That I loved Marco Ansaldo and Fabio Vergnano of *La Stampa*. That I loved Luciano Bertolani of the *Corriere dello Sport*, who was a bigger Lazio fan than Claudio Lotito. That I loved Paolo Forcolin of *La Gazzetta*. That I loved Vittorio Oreggia and Camillo Forte of *Tuttosport*. And that I loved Emanuele Gamba of *La Repubblica*, a claret-colored fan of Torino from head to foot, just like Aurelio Benigno, who wrote for a thousand different papers. Very simply, I thought of them as fellow adventurers. Over the years, I told a bushel of lies to journalists, too, but it was a survival technique. Between them and the three-headed monster, I often chose the three-headed monster. Still, that burst of applause was a sign of affection—the last good thing I remember from my time as the Juventus coach.

Not even the journalists were able to help me answer one question. And that one doubt remains even now: if the Triad had already rehired Lippi, why did they renew my contract anyway?

Envelope A: because we were on a tear for the championship season, and they wanted to keep my morale up and let me do my job without distractions.

Envelope B: they were about to acquire Buffon and Thuram from Parma, and I was on excellent terms with them.

Envelope C: they didn't want me to go to a major club like Milan, which is something that couldn't have happened anyway, since the *rossineri* had already picked Terim.

I never could make up my mind between envelopes A, B, and C. I never quite understood it, but maybe the solution of the puzzle is simpler than I thought. They tricked me, to keep me on their side. A stratagem to make me still feel I was the best.

The Dottore, however, attempted to give me an explanation, at least about why he decided not to renew my position as coach: "Ancelotti, you don't get along with people. There's a problem with the atmosphere." Okay, then maybe you should call Greenpeace. I never believed that. My theory? I think they fired me because I hadn't managed to win.

During my time coaching Juventus, I met one of the players who was destined to make me a success: the legendary Pippo. Pippo Inzaghi who, though he is pushing forty, still eats Plasmon biscuits. The discovery of the century. When I first arrived at Juventus, he was out of commission with a sports hernia. Still, we immediately hit it off; we had an instinctive understanding.

Pippo has always been something of an animal. If I think of the perfect striker, he's certainly not the first one to come to mind. He's an incomplete player. Still, inside the penalty area, no player on earth can compete with him. He woos and seduces the soccer ball. Inside that limited area, he scores in every way imaginable: striking with his right foot, his left foot, with cannon shots, ricochets, shots off the thigh, the shin, back heels, with eyes shut tight, shots off his ass (often off his ass), with his fingertip, goals off of penalty kicks gone astray, off his ear, his big toe, through mind control, and even with his shoelace. There are times when another player scores and he celebrates anyway. My favorite description of Inzaghi is by Emiliano Mondonico: "Is Pippo in love with goals? No, goals are in love with him." And it's a red-hot passion.

Inzaghi and Del Piero made a good pair, but they got along only in theory. The problem was always the usual problem between players. One of them was the least selfless player on earth (and I'm not talking about Ale)—a shortcoming that only reinforced Del Piero's standing as a great player. Now, it's not like Pippo and Ale fought all the time, but they weren't exactly in love either. The team locker room managed to sand down some of their rough edges. It was a hell of a locker room, tough to the point of brutality, with a roster of bad boys like Antonio Conte, Ciro Ferrara, and Gianluca

Pessotto. Not to mention Montero and Zidane. Ale and Pippo might not have been a dream couple—if anything, they looked more like a common-law couple, living under the same roof but without an excessive level of commitment. It wasn't an enduring love; they were both just punching the clock and making the union minimum.

That's how it was between me and Juventus: a love story that was over before it began. We were too different—different in every way. I was a boy from the country, they were managers—executives in jackets and ties. A Swatch up against three Rolexes—plastic versus gold. Still, I respected them from the very first to the very last day. When they sent me to Felegara for the winter, I didn't really suffer much. In fact, I didn't mind in the slightest. Often, when a door closes, the gate swings open. And just when you least expect it, off in the distance, with an awe-inspiring echo, you hear the voice of a chairman repeating a phrase you heard a few years earlier: "I want to win everything. We'll become the masters of Italy, Europe, and the world." Oh, Lord, he still hasn't stopped drinking.

Still, when Berlusconi calls, I can't help it; I'm there.

CHAPTER 19

How I Lost my Temper and Gained my A. C. Milan

Fatih Terim doesn't know it, but the reason that he was replaced at A. C. Milan was primarily culinary in nature. His downfall had a lot to do with the delicious Italian cold cut *culatello*. It was November 2001, just a few days after the Day of the Dead: in memoriam for the *Imparator*, relieved of his post and replaced by me. Galliani started laughing after he chose me as his new coach: "My dear Ancelotti, I'm happy."

"Thank you. Your expression of esteem fills me with joy."

"I was saying I'm happy because at last, with you, we can change the menu at Milanello."

In other words, Galliani had picked me because, with that other coach, the food was so bad. Maybe he'd found me in the Michelin guide: Trattoria Da Carletto, reservations suggested. Perhaps he decided to call ahead. "*Pronto*, this is Adriano. Could you add one guest to the party? We'll probably be ordering *culatello* and Felino salami for the whole table."

Maybe the most important consideration was that he could start guzzling wine again. Whenever Galliani orders a meal, there's plenty of wine.

Terim, in contrast, maintained a steady diet of thin broth and tap water, an intolerable affront to Galliani's senses. There was another thing: Terim was a *Big Brother* addict, so he'd often leave Galliani to finish lunch alone and run back to the privacy of his room, alone in front of the television set. He wanted to see if the people in the House were having sex. They did, as it happened—then Milan screwed *him*. To avoid any risk, when I signed the contract, I raised my right hand and put my left hand on my heart: "I swear that I'll always put A. C. Milan ahead of any and all cast members of *Big Brother*. Cross my heart."

In a not-too-distant past, for that matter, I had sworn an oath that one day I'd coach the *rossineri*. I had just started coaching Reggiana, and I was a guest at Sebastiano Rossi's wedding. In the church, I went over to Galliani and started whispering sweet blandishments in his ear: "Adriano, everything I do in the years to come will be nothing but an apprenticeship. One day, I'm going to coach A. C. Milan, and you're going to hire me."

"Well, I certainly hope so, Carletto. But now get your lips off my ear, please. It looks like we're the ones getting married."

It was like that time in Rome, at the Palazzo al Velabro, the first time we met. I was starting to develop a taste for this. Rossi was at the altar, exchanging vows; Galliani and I were just beginning our courtship.

I kept the promise I'd made. I went back to Milanello, and there was a bench waiting for me. Also waiting for me was the manager of the Milanello sports center, Antore Peloso: "Welcome back home, Carletto." Galliani was still there, such a permanent fixture that the answer to that persistent question is shrouded in the mists of time: Did Berlusconi build Adriano Galliani before he built Milanello? Which came first: his egg-shaped head or the hen that laid golden eggs? Over the years, I've gotten to know Galliani. He has red-and-black blood flowing through his veins. His mood and his very existence depend exclusively on the score at the end of the match. If A. C. Milan wins, then everything's fine. If they lose, then good luck to everyone. He's a manager with a desk; he's a soccer fan with a stadium—two souls compressed into a single body. Someone planned him out the way he is, without a wig. When A. C. Milan scores a goal, he is transfigured, he celebrates as if he were in a movie: *Poltergeist*. He's a first-class executive, extremely competent, unrivaled in his mastery of the art of administration. For the things that he has accomplished, the people of the Milan tribe should be eternally grateful. He is Berlusconi's right-hand and left-hand man: if the chairman is absent, Galliani is all too present.

Galliani and I have always enjoyed an excellent relationship; we've never exchanged harsh words, we've never been on terms of anything less than complete respect, even if over the years there have been arguments at times, always over the use of this player or that. There was one argument in particular, in Madrid, during my second season as coach. We were playing in the Champions League, and we'd already progressed into the second round. We were scheduled to play against Real Madrid. During training, I was trying out a formation filled with reserve players. Galliani watched without saying a word. Then we went back to the hotel and ate dinner. After the meal, he took me aside: "You aren't seriously planning to field that formation are you?"

"Well, actually, yes, I am."

"Then you've lost your mind."

"We've already passed that point, we need to think ahead to the championship season ..."

"We are A. C. Milan, and don't you ever forget it. Now, let me explain a thing or two."

He gave me a lesson in geography: "We're in Madrid."

A lesson in history: "Whoever wins here will be remembered for all time."

A lesson in religion: "The Estadio Santiago Bernabéu is a temple, a shrine."

And a lesson in philosophy: "Power consists of conviction, and I am deeply convinced that you are getting everything backward."

Last of all, he gave me a warning: "And remember, I'm not an idiot."

I'll keep that in mind. But, in the meantime, I'm sticking to my guns because, as I have mentioned once or twice before, I decide on the formation—me and nobody else. We lost, 3–1, and Galliani came charging back. With the usual warning, slightly modified from the pregame version: "And please remember, I am not an idiot"—even though the fans might have begged to differ, more than once, especially after the renewal of certain contracts for players who were certainly ready for retirement.

In reality, Galliani understood perfectly that the secret to making A. C. Milan a great team is the sense of loyalty and identification on the part of the players—a sense that required training, like everything else. The more time they spend together, the better. Pride goeth before a high ranking. Even old age can serve a valid purpose, within reason. The air that you breathe at Milanello is special, a mixture of oxygen and pixie dust; in your lungs you can feel the gratitude toward those who have given so much to this team. Galliani is always there, he never wavers, 24/7 he is at the service of A. C. Milan. That's passion, not work. Adriano Emergency Rescue Service: by day, by night, anytime.

Galliani worked closely with me from the beginning, from the instant I arrived. On a Monday, I signed the contract; on Tuesday I was introduced to the team; on Wednesday I moved into my office, the legendary Room Number 5, the first door when you climb the stairs from the front door at Milanello. It's the biggest office there, a bed on the left, bookshelves and a desk on the right, mini-fridge in a corner, and a heavy coating of history whatever direction you look. There's a balcony—vast, really a terrace—looking out over the fields; stand up, open the window, and you're on the job. If you have good eyesight, you can see even further and look into the future, because, all things considered, everything goes past that window and that desk. Everything that you can dream up at night, when you can't seem to fall asleep. Room Number 5 has always been the coach's office; the first time I walked into that room, I had a distinct impression. I could sense an array of presences. I was sleeping in the bed that had belonged to Nereo Rocco, Arrigo Sacchi, and Fabio Capello. And also Óscar Wáshington Tabárez, admittedly.

In the old days, Capello—under the influence, I believe, of the director of the sports center, Antore Peloso—used to claim that there was a ghost in Milanello, wandering freely down the hallways, especially after sunset. I never understood which was crazier, Don Fabio or that ghost, who had decided to pick on him of all people. It really got to be a problem. I can still see Capello, shoulders thrown back, chest swelling with righteous indignation, as if in an imitation of Antonio Cassano: "Begone! Go fuck yourself, evil spirit. This is not a team of dead men."

My A. C. Milan in that first year, though, was not that far removed from a team of the dead: it was sloppy, ill thought out, halfhearted. Along with Terim, the team had acquired a number of first-rate footballers, such as Inzaghi and Rui Costa, but first one then the other was injured. I had already played with Maldini, Costacurta, and Albertini, and that helped me out at first, at least in terms of relations.

It was a so-so season. The real story of that A. C. Milan began in Bologna. In the wake of a defeat: 2–0 in favor of the hosts of the game, while we were buried in shame. We played miserably. That match made me lose my temper in a way that hadn't happened in the previous eight years; for the first and (almost) the only time, I turned the locker room on its head in a bout of fury. I was looking at a team without enthusiasm, without motivation, without ambition, and I just couldn't hold my anger in. I slammed my fist down on the table, kicked the door with my foot, broke a bottle, and started to shout. I insulted everyone and everything. I attacked them on a personal level, I intentionally said cruel and abusive things, I reminded them that it's one thing to do something stupid, it's another thing to *be* stupid. Which is what they all seemed to be right then and there. That talk shook them up, and it changed the course of our history as a team, for the better. After that nightmarish ninety minutes, we were six points down from being in fourth place, just that far from the Champions League; at the end of the season, we came in fourth. But we lost Albertini, who decided to go in search of greener pastures after I benched him during the game against Juventus in Turin: "Carlo, I really didn't expect this from you. We've played together as teammates, I thought we had a different relationship. This marks the end of everything." He left, and I was sorry; it hurt me. He could have stayed as an alternative to Pirlo, who was just beginning to emerge.

At the end of that first year, we were playing with a 4-4-2 formation, and the starting lineup was as follows: Abbiati in goal; four-man defense with Contra, Laursen, Costacurta, and Maldini; Gattuso, Pirlo, Ambrosini, and Serginho in midfield; Shevchenko and Inzaghi up front. Many of the same names play from the first minute even today...

CHAPTER 20

King in England,
Thanks to the Christmas Tree

It was a holiday every day of the year during my second season on the bench for A. C. Milan. I was the gardener who worked on Christmas Day. You turn the soil here and plant your seeds there, and you come up with a great invention: the Christmas Tree formation. One goalkeeper, four defenders, three midfielders, two attacking midfielders, and a striker; when you see them all together on the field, they really do look like a fir tree—shiny baubles included, colored lights extra.

It was pure coincidence. The market had brought us Clarence Seedorf, Dario Šimić, and Rivaldo. After our victory in the early round of the Champions League against Slovan Liberec, we got Alessandro Nesta too. Shevchenko was injured, but Rivaldo,

Rui Costa, Seedorf, and Pirlo had to play. The club philosophy demanded it: beautiful football, first and foremost.

I got a lot of help from Pirlo, who came to see me in the locker room one fine day: "I can try to play as a defensive midfielder. I played that position with Mazzone, and it worked great." From one Carletto (Mazzone) to another (me). I had my doubts: I was afraid that Andrea Pirlo might create problems in terms of timing, because he likes to take the ball and keep it. A safe with a slow combination. I wasn't overly confident in this new approach, but I listened to him and gave it a try at the Berlusconi Trophy. I was astonished. He started playing with beautiful simplicity, and he became an unrivaled player. His name may have an unfortunate sound (*pirla* in Italian is an insult), but it's a name to conjure with.

And so it went until the away game against Deportivo de La Coruña in the UEFA Cup, a game in which A. C. Milan's genetic mutation came to completion. Deportivo's midfielders typically set the pace of the game, so in order to generate more space in the center of the field I told Rivaldo and Rui Costa to fall into more defensive positions. Inzaghi, further forward, was left unguarded, and he scored three goals. Our opponents were completely baffled: they weren't sure whether they should send a midfielder or a defender out against Rivaldo and Rui Costa. They lost their equilibrium, they left huge gaps for us to take advantage of; we were nimble, danced on through, and scored. Bullets and tap-dancing, 4–0 on our tiptoes. We were magnificent, and we began winning against teams all over Europe. Even in Munich against Bayern and in Dortmund against Borussia; Germany lay at our feet. I was proud to be Father Christmas: here, enjoy the contents of this

Christmas stocking. We were the team of December 25, always ready for a little celebration, whoever might happen along.

I'm proud of my invention. Our formation has even been translated into English: from *Albero di Natale* to Christmas Tree. I like the sound of that; it works for me. And it made us winners of the Champions League, though there was an element of sheer luck, because with Ajax in the quarterfinals we were out of the running: what saved us was a goal by Tomasson in the last minute: 3–2 in our favor, and the San Siro was packed. We played Internazionale in the semifinals: it was a real derby.

We had lost our determination in Serie A, so our focus was now on the European championship. We were under enormous pressure, and I could feel my bench starting to wobble dangerously. Finally, I felt at ease; the customary burning sensation on my buttocks helped me to get comfortable. In terms of physical conditions, there were beginning to be a few problems, and so I told the team to take a prudent approach: to keep from scoring goals. I'd even written it in the handouts I distributed during the last technical meeting, shortly before the game: "Ensure effective possession, avoid frenzy, don't carry the ball. Play two-touch football, and do your best to play deep behind the line of their midfielders whenever possible." Here's another one: "Don't be in a hurry, everyone should be involved in constructing the game, including the strikers. Bide your time, wait to find an opportunity for sudden counterattacks ... Play with confidence, remember that we're the stronger team, we have the better ideas."

I'm still an old-fashioned guy; I write everything by hand, even today—pen on paper, including the notes that I hand out to my players. It gives a touch of humanity to what I do; you can't write a love letter on a computer. That match ended with a score of 0–0, and I was happy about it. We had set aside a small advantage with a view to the return game, which we played the following week. I put pen to paper, and I prepared a second challenge for Inter. In among the technical suggestions and tactical tips, I added a heartfelt appeal: "This match is nothing more or less than the culmination of all our work, all our sacrifices. We should be happy that this moment has finally come." A note written at the bottom of the page, just before the assigned markings: Costacurta–Di Biagio, Nesta–Crespo, Maldini–Materazzi, Kaladze–Coco, Inzaghi–Cordoba, and Shevchenko–Cannavaro. In black ink on white paper, I also jotted down a list of the penalty takers, just because you can never be sure: Pirlo, Rui Costa, Seedorf, Inzaghi, Costacurta, Shevchenko, Nesta, Maldini, Kaladze, and Gattuso. We never needed them; we were satisfied with the 1–1 scoreline. The final seven minutes, from when Martins evened the score to the end of the game, were the longest minutes of my life. Time seemed to stand still, my heart was racing, I probably actually had a heart attack without even realizing it. In the end, all that passes, too. Most importantly, *we* passed. Old Trafford, here we come. To the Theater of Dreams, against Juventus. An insane final.

When I have to deal with situations of this kind, I rely on two principles: clarity and concentration. A few days before the game, instead of holding the usual technical meeting, I organized a sort of cineforum. I showed the players a scene from *Any Given Sunday*, the movie in which Al Pacino, as the coach of a football team, delivers an incredible speech just before a crucial game:

"You find out that life is just a game of inches. So is football. Because in either game—life or football—the margin for error is so small. And either we heal now, as a team, or we will die as individuals." Sends chills up and down your spine. On the night before the game, I took it a step further. I prepared a DVD showing every step of our charge toward Manchester: music, exultation, goals. It was us, our team, running headlong toward heaven. At the end I turned on the lights and I didn't say much: "There's just one more thing we need now." I would have nominated myself for an Oscar, for best screenplay.

Absolutely the last technical meeting was held at our training grounds just before we left for Old Trafford. All the players were there, in tracksuits, with a companion dressed slightly better than them—a little more elegant and distinguished. It was Silvio Berlusconi. He sat in the middle of the team, he wanted to take part. The fact that he was there made quite an impression on me. I handed out sheets of paper with the formations and the plays; he wanted copies for himself. (Later, I saw them published in a book by Bruno Vespa; the chairman passed them off as his own, but fair enough, because before every game in the finals, he always gave our morale a huge boost.) Berlusconi sat listening to the positions I was assigning to the team. If I know anything about him at all, he was wishing I'd send him out onto the field—as part of the starting lineup, of course. I was worried, I was afraid I'd said something idiotic. At the end of the meeting, I even asked him: "How did I do, Mr. Chairman?"

"Beautifully, Carletto, you were great. You'll see, we're going to win."

And that's exactly what happened, with a camouflaged Christmas Tree; let's call it a slightly dirty 4-4-2, with Rui Costa on the right and Seedorf inside, moving actively around the field. We became European champions at the last penalty kick, even though it wasn't as easy as you might think to find players willing to take that penalty kick. If I think of the lineup of penalty takers, even now I get the chills: the first was Serginho, followed by Seedorf, Kaladze, Nesta, and, fifth, Shevchenko. Inzaghi had vanished; we couldn't find him, he'd simply dematerialized. I listed him as sixth, but we didn't need him. Shevchenko was decisive. Luckily, incredible but true, Juventus managed to put together a lineup that was even worse: Trezeguet, Birindelli, Zalayeta, Montero, and Del Piero. A second before Shevchenko kicked, I thought: "Okay, it's over." Then it happened. A second later—and this is what I'll never forget—it was incredible to see the entire Juventus end of the stands motionless. It looked like a poster. I wanted to take it off the wall and carry it home with me, but unfortunately I didn't have a wall big enough to hang it on. In any case, my dear Milan fans, best wishes from the everlasting instant. What enormous satisfaction.

At four in the morning, I was scarfing down my second bowl of pasta all'amatriciana, prepared for me by Oscar Basini, our team chef. At five in the morning, we were all drunk in the hotel, completely snookered on English beer. We went out and started playing soccer on the hotel golf course, tearing up the green. The hotel staff was distraught: they were tempted to toss us out, but they couldn't. We were the masters of all Europe, and so, for that one magical night, we were the masters of Manchester as well. We wanted to be considerate—we'd taken all possible precautions, we had even decided to take off our shoes to keep from ruining the green—but accidents happen. Even barefoot, Gattuso is a bulldozer. He tore up everything, even the hole in the middle of the green. In the meantime, Galliani had taken away the cup. He had locked himself in his hotel room with it. He'd taken the Champions League to bed with him. The poor little thing.

CHAPTER 21

Kaká, the Greatest
Unknown Player on Earth

Another round, another gift. An incredible, wonderful gift. Completely unexpected. You should never look a gift horse in the mouth, that much is certain. But after you've untied the bows and unwrapped it, you can certainly thank heaven. And you can thank the horse. That seems to me the very least you can do. Summer 2003 is when that horse—no, more like that Martian— landed. Scholars of extraterrestrial life, lend me your ears: We are pleased to introduce you to Kaká—an absolute world premiere. A child prodigy at play on the fields of the European champions.

I had certainly heard something about a young man from Brazil, a pretty talented kid, but I didn't know anything more than that: a certain Ricardo Izecson dos Santos Leite. From the name, if I had to guess, I would have assumed he was a young preacher, and, in a way, I was pretty near the mark. He was spreading the gospel of soccer and faith: Listen to his word and you shall discover eternal bliss. The club wasn't sure whether to invite him to come to Milanello immediately or else leave him to mature in Saõ Paulo for another six months. After thinking it over, we decided to speed up the process, to bring him over as soon as possible to allow him to train with us—and to let me get an idea of just who we were dealing with. As far as I could tell, we were buying something with our eyes closed, based on a lot of pretty promises and a frothy tide of high hopes. That's all well and good, but what I need is concrete evidence.

Kaká landed at Milan's Malpensa Airport, and I felt like pulling out tufts of my hair: he was wearing schoolboy glasses, his hair was neatly brushed, he had the scrubbed, rosy-cheeked face of a straight-A student. All he lacked was a book bag and a lunchbox. Oh, Lord, what have we done? He's not ready to pick a major, much less play professional soccer. Welcome to the international exchange student program; now let's find out if you even know how to dribble and kick.

Kaká looked nothing like a Brazilian footballer; if anything, he looked like a Jehovah's Witness in the industrial belt outside Milan. I started asking around, and everyone told me the same thing: "Sure, he has potential. He's an attacking midfielder, but he's not superfast. If he plays in an Italian championship game, he could run into trouble when things get tight." I'm going to keep the names of my sources confidential, to keep from making them look like donkeys.

In the meantime, Moggi began lobbing grenades from Turin, and the shrapnel all spelled out the same general notion: "With that nickname, he's done for in Italy, it's like calling him Poopy." "We don't need to go caca OR Kaká." "At Juventus, we're all constipated." "We're the Triad, and we don't pay good money for stinky Kaká." It was like a vaudeville act, and I started to have a sneaking sense of doubt: just wait and see, maybe Lucianone is right about this one too. It wouldn't be the first time.

I had never seen Kaká play, even on video. So I was worried, more than a little. One day, during a press conference, someone asked me about him, about his gifts and skills, about what we expected from him. And they wanted more: human interest, details, anecdotes, and future prospects. It was an in-depth interview on a subject I hadn't studied in the slightest, about which I knew nothing. It was an exam that I could only hope to flunk. I did my best to muddle through, recycling stories I'd heard from others, and one-size-fits-all generalities: "He has two legs, he wears football boots with studs and heels, he's a soccer player by vocation and profession . . ."—that kind of stuff. It was awkward. "He's a good midfielder, he can play in a more attacking position, too. You might call him slow, he has a nice personality. In short, he reminds me a little of Toninho Cerezo." I had played with Cerezo, and, from the descriptions I'd heard of Kaká, the comparison might hold up. I just took a stab in the dark, but nobody seemed to have caught on. That's the way it always is at press conferences: you fake it, you spout blatant nonsense, and everybody nods wisely. Even the people who work with you.

At last, one fine day, Kaká showed up for training. For orientation. The first thing I wanted to do was ask him, "Now, have you told your mother and father you won't be going to school today?" Milanello security would certainly have had fair cause to ask to see his driver's license before letting him in. But what happened next is this: still groggy from jet lag, he got onto the field, and I heard a heavenly choir and the sound of trumpets. He was a heaven-sent genius, truly sent by heaven. So, if I may: thank you, Lord. Thank you.

Once he got the ball between his feet, he was incredible. I stopped talking, because there were no words to express what I was feeling. There were just no words in my vocabulary for what I was seeing. Truly superior stuff.

In his first clash as a member of A. C. Milan, Kaká found himself face-to-face with Rino Gattuso, who gave him a violent shoulder block, massive but not sufficient to make Kaká lose control of the ball. Rino took it with admirable calm, enlightening us with a profound observation about that little encounter: "Aw, go fuck yourself." In his way, he had just put the team's seal of approval on his new teammate. That teammate, after holding onto the ball, gave it a tremendous smack, easily thirty yards, to the frustration of Nesta, who completely failed to block it. Now, hold on for a second, this doesn't make sense. Give me that remote control, I want to watch the replay. I had TiVo, I just didn't know it yet. My dear Moggi, maybe it's because I'm a congenital overeater, but I like Kaká. I really like him. A lot. He takes off his glasses, puts on a pair of shorts, and he becomes something I never would have expected: a world-class player.

After every training session, Galliani and I would talk on the phone. I'd tell him everything that was going on, the things that had happened, and he would give me his thoughts and impressions. It was an uninterrupted daily relationship. That day, I called him: "Signore Galliani, I have some news for you."

"Good news or bad?"

"Good news. Excellent news."

"Carletto, are you quitting?"

He felt like joking—always a positive sign. "No, I'm staying, and one of the reasons is that we have just acquired a phenomenon."

He might not be at Zidane's level, but he was close. He was the second greatest player I've ever coached, and certainly the most intelligent. He understands things on the fly, he thinks twice as fast as the others; when he receives the ball, he's already figured out how the play is going to end. The following training sessions were just like the first. The third, the fourth, the fifth: they were all the same—a spectacle with a happy ending.

I wasn't the only one who was impressed with Kaká; he'd also made quite an impression on his teammates. All of them. And you can imagine how many magnificent footballers they'd seen passing through. He'd even made a strong impression on Maldini, who, to mention just one name, had played with Marco van Basten. From the swan of Utrecht to the young preacher of São Paulo. Kaká immediately made friends with Gattuso. They became very close, and soon they began kidding around. Oil and water—or, perhaps, devil's oil and holy water—they made an unlikely but magnificent pair. (Just to make clear what a character he was, Gattuso once ate a live snail at Milanello during a training session.)

Over the last few years, the scenario has pretty much remained the same. Kaká runs toward Gattuso. Gattuso runs toward Kaká. They seem to see one another at a distance, and then move inevitably closer, like a shootout in a Western. They may not have holstered pistols, but they start their duels with mockery. In general, Ricky is the first to speak: "You uncouth southern peasant." Rino doesn't say a word, but he chases after him, catches him, and swings a straight-armed slap at the back of his head. Kaká must have been head-slapped a thousand times since he arrived. A normal person would be completely dazed and dizzy, but it is Kaká's good fortune that he is normal only in terms of manners and appearance. Otherwise, he does things on a regular basis that others frequently have a hard time even thinking.

Pato made quite an impression on me the first time I saw him play, too, but nothing like what happened with Kaká. I got to know Pato over time, one training session after another, but with Ricardo it was a bolt from the blue—a sudden and total conversion. What immediately struck me about Pato was his sheer speed; he's a hundred-meter sprinter on a soccer field. What struck me about Kaká was, simply, everything. Every single thing. My Lord, what a soccer player You sent down to us here on earth. The day he arrived, he completely changed A. C. Milan, for the quite reasonable fee of eight million dollars. A dream, at a bargain-basement price.

In a fairly static team—Rui Costa and Rivaldo generally played with the ball between their feet—we tampered with the speedometer. Now we were traveling much faster than the machine was designed to go. Kaká was extraordinarily dynamic, although we were bounced out of the 2003–04 Champions League when we lost a disastrous match at La Coruña, in the Italian championship season we basically had no rivals. It was a stroll in the park. We were the champions of Italy, thanks to a player I'd never heard of. And there is one thing for which Kaká never forgave me: "Coach, I have to ask, had you lost your mind that day? You compared me to Cerezo..." And indeed the two players have absolutely nothing in common, but that day at the press conference, I couldn't know that yet. All of the strongest soccer teams on earth have always followed Kaká, and rightly so: there are no other players like him on the circuit. The sheikhs want him. So do the *merengues*. So does Chelsea. A universal object of desire, and, as such, he is now expensive—very expensive.

When Kaká joined Milan, he immediately helped us win the Scudetto. Immediately. Galliani celebrated, but he didn't take the Italian tricolor cup to bed. He'd left his heart in Manchester; he could never forget his night of passion with the European Cup, because the Champions League is more important than anything else. There's only one class of people who would disagree with me: those who haven't been able to win it.

CHAPTER 22

The Truth from Istanbul:
You Have to Fall to Rise Again

That evening, May 25, 2005, there was excitement in the locker room at Atatürk Stadium in Istanbul. It was a joyous half-time. The first half of the Champions League final had just come to an end, and we were beating Liverpool, 3–0: we had played flawless soccer. One goal by Maldini, two by Crespo; here comes the cavalry. Just forty-five more minutes, and we would become the champions of all Europe, the highest peak of that season. Give us back the European Cup, and we'll take it home with us. Add a place setting for dinner, we have a new girlfriend. The players started urging one another on, aloud: "Come on, we can win this"; "Let's go boys, this is happening"; "We're winning, we're winning, we're winning."

They were clapping and cheering. We weren't counting our chickens, we were just getting revved up, filled with positive energy. That happens. In the little dressing room next door, the players I had sent up into the stands were putting on our victory shirts under their team uniforms. Our victory—a victory that, however, remained to be won.

The air was sparkling and cool, which seemed appropriate. A. C. Milan, ready for the bubbly. So I let the team vent and applaud for a few minutes, then I told them to calm down: "Look, when you're playing against Brits, a match is never really over, so let's be careful here. Let's make sure they don't seize control at the beginning of the second half. We can't, and we shouldn't, collapse. Let's manage our control of the ball and our control of the game. Go! Go, Milan!" That was my speech. Nothing more, nothing less.

That evening, Liverpool had begun the match with a single striker, Baroš, which is why I would have expected Cissé to come onto the field at the beginning of the second half. It didn't happen. Strange tactics Rafa Benítez was employing. And, in fact, everything looked great for us when the game resumed; we came close to ratcheting the score up to 4–0. Then, the unforeseeable happened: a six-minute blackout. The impossible became possible. ("Impossible is nothing" is a slogan that I've always hated, because it turned ugly on us that day.) We were our own worst nightmare. The world turned upside down. The second and minute hands of my watch started twirling in the wrong direction: ladies and gentlemen, we're running on disaster time now. We were hurtling into the dreamworld of the English bookmakers, and well beyond. If we had bet against ourselves, we would have become richer than we already were. The score: 3–1; 3–2; 3–3. I couldn't believe it. This couldn't be happening. I was paralyzed, and I didn't even have time to react. I was baffled; nothing made sense. Who could have kept their senses? In the course of just 360 seconds, destiny had changed the direction of the match, twirling it 180 degrees. A complete change of course, an inexorable and continuous decline. The light had gone out, and there was no time to change the bulb. It was moving too fast, there was no chance to run for shelter. A perfect piece of machinery in an irreversible nosedive. Incredible but true.

People often ask me what went through my mind during Liverpool's recovery. The answer is simple: nothing. Zero. My brain was a perfect vacuum, the vacuum of deep space. I did my best to focus, to concentrate. We went into overtime and finally started playing like the team we were, the team we believed we were, the team that still could, and had to, beat Liverpool. Even then, deep down, I still hoped to pull it off. Right up to the very last minute, when Dudek made a miracle save against Shevchenko. Andriy headed the ball toward goal, and we were already celebrating sweet victory, but the goalkeeper managed to block the shot. Andriy regained possession of the ball, and Dudek blocked it again, just as he was getting back up from the ground. Corner kick. Ouch. It was then, and only then, that I began to see ghosts—not until then. My brain began functioning again, and I managed to put together a complete and coherent thought: "This is starting to look bad."

In the meantime, the match had gone into a penalty shootout. I looked my players in the eyes, and I saw that something had gone wrong. They were overthinking it all. And right before you're about to kick from the penalty mark, that's never a good attitude to have. At that point, I was practically certain we were done for. And to think that the designated penalty kickers, unlike what had happened at Manchester against Juventus, were our good ones: Serginho, Pirlo, Tomasson, Kaká, and Shevchenko. When I saw Dudek dancing before each one of our penalty kicks to try to shake our concentration, I was reminded of the final that we, Roma, lost to Liverpool in a penalty shootout. There, too, Grobbelaar, on the goal line, had done a creditable imitation of a hysterical belly dancer. One no better than the other, him and Dudek. In the locker room after the game, I had very little to say: "In moral terms, we won that game. If we do our best, someday we'll have this opportunity again..."

I never watched that match again, and I never will. Not so much because of the pain, but simply because there is no point to it. I feel no need to watch it again. Now I think of the disaster of Istanbul as a loss like any other. My depression has lifted. Of all the players, Crespo is probably the one who took it the hardest; he'd never won a European Cup, and that evening in Turkey he thought his time had come—a feeling that only grew during the game, after he scored not one but two goals. For his effort and his gifts, he really deserved to go home with a major piece of recognition. Even today, he lives with the regret that he was unable to hoist that Champions League cup; he deserved it more than all the others.

Crespo had begun that season as a cadaver, and he ended it as a hero. He had improved vastly, and all credit was due to him. When we acquired him in the summer from Chelsea, he was another man: ungainly, slow, depressed, he no longer seemed like a soccer player at all. (I still don't know what they did to him.) He couldn't even score; he didn't get his first goal until November, in the Italian Cup games. He worked like crazy to recover, and, in the end, he succeeded. It was the old Crespo again, the one I'd known from my time at Parma. My prize student, my good close friend.

One step down, in the ranks of despair, was Gattuso, who was ready to leave A. C. Milan after the match against Liverpool. Some kind of psychic sinkhole had opened up inside him, sucking him down into darkness.

Then, all together, we came to a conclusion, even though it took us some time: we would return in triumph precisely because of that crushing defeat. Just when that would be, we still couldn't say. We couldn't possibly know. First, we had to gather up all the shattered pieces of us, ourselves, and our team, and reassemble them. It was the most complicated puzzle I ever faced. It was in that period that I went back to find the thesis I had written for my master's degree at Coverciano to become a fully accredited, first-class soccer coach. I flipped through the pages, going directly to the chapter on psychology:

> … one outcome of this lack of results is that the player begins to feel a waning enthusiasm, with the risk of calling into question the effectiveness of the work that he is being asked to do. The coach—with the support of the club, of course—must have faith in his ideas, must keep from wavering, must remain confident in his convictions, but, above all, must be aware that he has a group of players that is following

him and approves his choices and decisions. If you are sure that the group is on your side, then that is the time to insist on the work that must be done.

Another one:

… you must take care to avoid creating anxiety in the pursuit of results at all costs; this is harmful and counterproductive, if you wish to obtain a high level of performance. If the group manages to overcome this series of difficulties, then it becomes more cohesive and much more powerful. At that time, a coach knows that he can count totally on players who are united, highly motivated, and determined. When you can count on a group of people with these characteristics, the work will be less tiresome and the results will certainly be more noteworthy.

I may have been a bad writer, but apparently the prescription for the team's crisis was always clear to me. Tragedy can only produce better performance. Either you emerge, all rowing in the same direction, or you're done for.

The process of psychological reconstruction is a lengthy one, perhaps even too long. It took us the entire 2005–06 season to complete it. We didn't win a thing that year—an unusual situation for our group of players and one we'd never experienced before.

While I'm on the subject, let me say something about a notion that is of interest to many people I've spoken to: perhaps the decline of Alberto Gilardino—who had just joined the team—began at this very point. Alberto is a somewhat fragile personality, and it wasn't the dream of his life to be acquired by a club like

A. C. Milan in the midst of such a troubled period. He was crushed by the ensuing pressure.

In any case, we emerged from the ordeal stronger. I may be crazy, but I think that the defeat at Istanbul wasn't completely negative. It had its reasons and its value. We were ready to start over from scratch. All together, hand in hand, into the eye of the hurricane. The hurricane of the Italian soccer scandal: Calciopoli.

CHAPTER 23

An Impatient Pinocchio

The nose. It's long—incredibly long. In the summer of 2006, Pinocchio had come to terms with us; he was practically a member of the A. C. Milan team. We even had his uniform ready. Ready for Zlatan Ibrahimović, the perfect striker, arriving from the distant shores of Juventus. Perfect in and of himself, and perfect for my team. An assault weapon in my hands, with the ammunition clip entrusted to Kaká. In my imagination, I was already training him, the tempered-steel tip of our little Christmas Tree.

The problem was that Ibra lacked the strength of character to wait patiently. Haste makes waste, but Massimo Moratti pays good money; so one more world-class soccer player went to Inter. It disappointed me. This was the first sting of the Calciopoli scandal, and, more than ointment, I needed a suit of armor to deal with what followed. In the summer of 2006, Ibra had been our major designated purchase, but we didn't yet know whether we would be playing in Serie A or Serie B. He certainly didn't want to drop down a ranking. So we asked him to give us a little more time until it became clear. He didn't have any more time to give us, apparently. He changed his plans and his colors without changing his city. Too bad. He wanted to win the Champions League; we could have served that to him on a silver platter just a year later.

I was to console myself over our loss with a new acquaintance, Warrant Officer Auricchio, the great discovery of that period. Every day I read sensational new reports in the daily press; from time to time, the versions would change, usually for the worse. A. C. Milan in Serie A; Milan in Serie B; it could even go down to Serie C; Milan won't be penalized; Milan will be penalized; Milan is going to compete in the Champions League; Milan out of the running for the European Cup; Milan guilty; Milan very guilty. I was ready at this point for anything, even the revelation that Galliani had assassinated JFK. It was the end of the world.

One day I was at home with a group of friends; we were talking about everything that was happening. I said I was amazed that the police hadn't called me yet. They were questioning everyone they could think of. As if by stage direction, my cell phone rang at that very moment. It was from an unlisted number, caller unknown, which is like the signature of the classic prankster: "Hello, this is the carabinieri of Rome, I'm Warrant Officer Auricchio."

"Oh, come on. You trying to pull my leg? Who is this?"

"Sir, believe me, I'm telling you the truth. I really am Warrant Officer Auricchio."

Sure, Auricchio, like the brand of provolone cheese. Mmmm-mmm ... Auricchio—tastes good, and good for you!

"Look, you can give me all the plausible details you want, my dear Auriemma...."

"Auricchio!"

"Sure, right—Auricchio. But your surname is obviously a little too cute. I'm pretty sure this is a prank call."

My friends were all there; I wondered which one was trying to fool me by arranging for this anonymous prank call. "Listen, Ancelotti, this is serious business; we need to talk."

"Sure, but I don't know who you are."

"My name is Auricchio."

"Again? I got that part. I just don't know who you really are."

"This is the carabinieri of Rome."

"What is this, a broken record? If this really is the carabinieri of Rome, send me something official—a warrant, a radiogram."

"Ancelotti, the Italian police haven't used radiograms since World War II."

"Listen, Auriemma ..."

"Auricchio!"

"Right, okay, Auricchio, send me anything you want, but I want something from you to prove that you're telling the truth. How about this: send a fax to the carabinieri in my hometown, and they can contact me."

I addressed him with the informal "*tu*," while Auricchio continued to use the formal "*Lei*." Something didn't really make sense; as a prank, it was verging on the excessive.

"Signor Ancelotti, you are a public figure. We'd really prefer to keep this private and confidential. It's for your own good. Come to Rome in two days."

"Why would I want to come to Rome? Will you cut this out or not? What do you want from me? Who is this, anyway?"

"This is Auricchio."

We sounded like Jiminy Cricket and Pinocchio. Or maybe Tweedle-Dee and Tweedle-Dum, because Pinocchio was already training over at Internazionale.

"Listen, Ancelotti, let's do this. I'll call you back in two or three days."

"Do as you like."

"*Buon giorno*, Ancelotti."

"*Buon giorno*, Auriemma, or whatever the fuck your name is."

I had induced an identity crisis in the poor policeman. I was increasingly certain that it was all a joke, partly because the timing was just too perfect. Auricchio had called me at the exact moment in which I was talking about the investigation with my friends.

Just out of curiosity, I started asking around. And it turns out there really was a Warrant Officer Auricchio. Even worse: he was a big wheel, a major figure in the ongoing investigation. I suddenly imagined myself in handcuffs, being indicted for insulting a public officer in the pursuit of his duties, moving steadily away from the coach's bench of Milan, and closer toward a bench in the prison of San Vittore. A bench that maybe didn't even wobble.

In the end, I had to go to Rome to the carabinieri barracks. Once I got there, a young man with short dark hair was waiting for me. It was him, the original, the one, the only, the inimitable Warrant Officer Auricchio. And he was really a very nice guy.

"Pleasure to meet you, I'm Ancelotti."

"The pleasure's all mine, I'm Auriemma."

"Auriemma?"

"No, what am I saying? Auricchio."

We enjoyed a jolly laugh, and it was the last. From then on, everything turned serious, damned serious.

He accompanied me into a room. There sat the investigating magistrates, Narducci and Beatrice, on one side of the table with a third person. I was on the other side of the table: just like back in school at finals. They were the professors, and I was the student. Or perhaps I should say the person of interest, the subject of the interrogation. Because I was a person with knowledge of the events, I couldn't just say whatever came into my mind, or I could have been charged with perjury. I had to tell the truth, and that is what I did. In particular, they asked me about the years I spent at Juventus, and whether I knew anything about Moggi's relations with referees. I also listened to a wiretap of Leonardo Meani, the former chief of referees at Milan, who was talking with the chief of the assistant referees after a Siena–Milan match in which he had disallowed a regulation goal by Shevchenko. In that conversation, Meani complained about the treatment we were getting. At a certain point, he had said, "I have Ancelotti here in the car with me." And that is why I was now sitting in a room with Auricchio. They let me go after about an hour.

The second deposition was held in the investigations office of the Federation, again in Rome, and it was no fun at all. I left there with the distinct impression that they had it in for Milan. They took a tough attitude with me, their questions about Meani (who was and remains a close friend of mine) were pressing; they were doing their best to establish direct involvement on the club's part. They almost seemed to take it for granted that we were guilty. I was very clear with the people who were questioning me: "Meani made those phone calls to protect A. C. Milan, to keep us from being continually penalized by specific calls by the referees." In other words, no one had done anything illegal or scandalous. I knew we hadn't done anything wrong, but we still had to suffer. I talked a lot with Galliani; he was very upset, the club's public image was at stake. The situation just drove him into a fury. To reassure him, I said, "I'm staying, even if they bump us down into Serie B." And the players with me.

In the end, we started eight points down in Serie A and from the preliminaries in the Champions League. Even today, I still believe that A. C. Milan was the victim of a terrible injustice. If we go back and closely examine the championship games in question, we certainly had no advantage over Juventus. If anything, it was the opposite, especially in the direct confrontations; on one occasion in Turin, the referee, Bertini, refused to allow two blindingly obvious penalties. He also disallowed the advantage rule when Kaká was still on his feet after being fouled while running toward our opponents' goal. We were three against one, and the referee stopped play. Three against two, if you include Bertini. That time, they really took it too far: the perfect crime.

The summer of Calciopoli was a terrible time: we, as an Italian team, were world champions with a giant blot against our name. The Italian tricolor in the mud. For A. C. Milan, there was the preliminary round of the European Cup against Red Star Belgrade, and we needed to train and prepare. So I was forced to call all the players to Milanello early. Including the players who had just played the final against France in Berlin. I remember my conversation with Inzaghi: "Pippo, I'm sorry, but you have to come back. We need you."

"Okay, coach, just give me a second."

It really did just take a second; in fact, Pippo seemed to beam down to the training camp. He set a fine example for everyone— even for Pinocchio.

CHAPTER 24

There Is No Such Thing
as the Malta Pact

If the Great Communicator, He who Knows, the Lord of the Press Conference, the Immense Provocateur, the Special Coach who never has to ask (although he was asked repeatedly about the Champions League at Chelsea, and seemed to offer no reply) had already been among us common mortals at the time, at the end of that cursed summer of 2006, he would certainly have stuck his nose into our business. And he would have said just one thing, with a Portuguese accent: "*Zeru tituli* for A. C. Milan." Zero titles, no championships, no trophies on the horizon.

In reality, though, we were getting ready to make our move. Granted, we had drafted Daniele Bonera for the preliminary rounds of the Champions League, only to discover that he had been disqualified and wouldn't be able to play. But otherwise all was good. We were, as usual, a trifle old, but actually in pretty good shape—Cafu in particular. He had surprised me. He showed up at Milanello just three days before the away game against Red Star, and he was in extraordinary condition. Every time he came back from Brazil, he looked like a brand new defender, fully rejuvenated. I never understood exactly what he did during his holidays, and I'm not sure I want to know. We won at home, and we won again at the away game; we qualified, and the Champions League couldn't go on without us. And we couldn't go on without the Champions League.

In that period, I was coaching two teams: officially, A. C. Milan, and in my heart, Liverpool. I was rooting for us and for them; I wanted to take both teams to the final match, which would be played in Greece. Over the previous year and a half, we had been knocked off track in Istanbul and by Calciopoli, and we had barely managed to qualify for the Champions rounds, but I was already thinking of Athens. I revealed my thoughts on the eve of the away game against AEK Athens, while I was being interviewed at the Olympic Stadium: "I'm here to get acquainted with the field." I remember that one or two older journalists—the kind that always think they know everything but really know less than the others—looked at me as if I was the village idiot. In fact, we struggled for a few more months after that. We gave up on the Italian championship almost immediately: being penalized eight points was just too much. In the Champions League, we were clumsy and not entertaining to watch. In the first round, we went up against AEK Athens, Anderlecht, and Lille. We got to the next level, but without generating a lot of excitement. In November and December, they were already giving us up for dead. *Zeru tituli. Zeru tituli.* The truth is that the engine was flooding: that summer, we hadn't had time to train properly, and that was beginning to weigh us down, to affect our play on the field. We couldn't wait for it to be Christmas so we could stop and recharge our batteries. But there was one piece of good news: Liverpool wasn't giving up. It was continuing its march; it was still in the running for the Cup, just like us. Everything was going according to plan—plans established by fate, not by me. Obviously, my bench was wobbling and swaying as if it were high on ecstasy, and Galliani had his monkey wrench out and was already loosening bolts: the vice president as a working man.

And so on, until the mid-season break. At that point, the club decided to take all of us to train in Malta: "At least you can get into good physical and athletic shape." There, we were reborn as a team; we started moving at a decent pace. We looked like a brand new squad, and, before long, people started talking about the notorious Malta Pact. So notorious, in fact, that it never existed. I don't even know what it was supposed to be. The newspapers all wrote the same phrases: "The Pact, The Team's Secret to Regaining Its Greatness." Those articles aroused my curiosity. So I asked the players about them. I was worried that they might have cut me out of the loop: "You haven't made some kind of pact without telling me, have you?" They didn't get it; they figured I must have gone senile. The reality was much simpler: we were working well, better than we ever had in the previous months. The same thing was happening at Liverpool: another piece of good news. I was asking around, following the news, keeping up on how they were doing. Viva the Reds.

In the meantime, Rino Gattuso was losing his mind, and it was all Kakha Kaladze's fault. Rino's birthday is January 9. A few days before his birthday, at the beginning of a training session, Kakha made us all stop what we were doing. He asked if he could speak. "Coach, sorry, I have something to say. It's very important."

"Be my guest, Kakha..."

"It's three days to Rino Gattuso's birthday."

Maybe his gears were starting to slip, but we decided to act as if nothing had happened. That night, at dinner, the same thing: "Excuse me, boys, I have something to tell you all."

"Go ahead, Kakha..."

"It's two days and fourteen hours till Rino Gattuso's birthday."

Our doctors gave us worried looks; they wanted to intervene, they were standing by with a straitjacket, cleaned and pressed, but we told them to hold off. The following morning, the same thing again. He raised his hand, and I let him go ahead: "Go ahead, Kakha..."

"It's two days until Rino Gattuso's birthday."

Poor Kaladze, Alzheimer's is a terrible thing. And in such a young man, too. The team members started laughing, and Rino started to lose his temper. He felt he was a target of ridicule. The countdown went on—and on, and on. Until the night of January 8: "Boys, it's just three hours until Rino Gattuso's birthday." Rino was having a hard time controlling himself at this point. He would have gladly beaten him within an inch of his life. Finally, it was the ninth: nothing. Zero. No one said a thing. The silence of the darkest days. So I finally spoke up: "Kakha, you don't by any chance have something to tell us?"

"No, coach, what on earth would I have to tell you?"

"You're sure you're not forgetting anything?"

"I don't think so."

I looked at Rino out of the corner of my eye; he was ticking like a time bomb, ready to go off at any second. He kept control of himself and believed he had emerged the winner. On January 10, at lunch at training camp, Kaladze came over to me with a very sad expression on his face. It seemed like something terrible had happened, so I walked over to him with a show of concern, and asked him, "Is there something wrong?"

"Yes, coach, it's three hundred and sixty-four days till Rino Gattuso's birthday."

Explosion in the cafeteria; we were clearly in the presence of a genius. He was immediately chased down by Rino and pummeled furiously. I think that this is when Kakha began to feel the first creakings in his knee. Maybe someone talked to the journalists about Kaladze, especially the older ones, who always claim to know everything but who had just got it wrong once again. It was Malta Cracked, not the Malta Pact.

Which, let me say it again, never existed—even though, in that period, I was beginning to pick up positive signals from the team. Or rather, from the teams: A. C. Milan and Liverpool. In everything I said, I emphasized the concept of how we had been penalized, the injustices to which we had been subjected, and how much I would like to give the lie to the birds of ill omen that hovered around us. My mind was free, so ideas entered my head more easily: "Boys, don't worry, I'm taking you to the final."

It was January, and I was still thinking about Athens. In the meantime, Massimo Ambrosini was thinking of quitting soccer entirely, because of his succession of injuries. His morale was so low that it had emerged on the far side of the globe. We were forced to undertake a major psychological project focusing on him—an attempt to change his mind-set, remind him of how much we needed him. It was important for us, for Liverpool—for everyone.

I had a clear idea of the ideal formation for us to win the Champions League, and he was part of that formation. "With you, we can win," I told him. The only reason he didn't tell me to go fuck myself was that he was a polite young man, but he was certainly on the verge of summoning an exorcist. But I insisted: "Massimo, I'm not kidding. Certain games, I can't send in Inzaghi and Gilardino together; we'd be too unbalanced. I want to dust off the good old Christmas Tree, and we need you there for it. End of story."

This was my idea: Gattuso, Pirlo, and Ambrosini in the middle; Kaká and Seedorf as a pair of attacking midfielders; and a single striker up front. Without Yoann Gourcuff, who was talented but also crazy. A strange, very strange young man, a little egocentric: he mostly thought about himself. He had incredible potential, but he kept it all to himself. Off the field, he was a troublemaker, but that never influenced my decisions. Very simply, he just didn't know how to fit in as a team player. In contrast, Ambrosini, who was playing in the Italian Cup again after a long period on the bench, felt a sharp pain in his thigh and slipped back into a kind of athletic depression: "That's it, I want to quit, I really can't take it anymore. I just don't think I can go on like this."

The doctor was baffled. He took me aside and practically whispered to me: "Look, he's fine. There's nothing wrong with his leg that I can see."

So I had another conversation with Massimo: "On Sunday, we're playing a championship match against Lazio. The doctors tell me that you're a hypochondriac, but you claim you are in pain. So let's do this. I'm going to field you, you keep playing as long as you can—a minute, two minutes, ten minutes, or even thirty. And if you break something, all the better; we'll solve the problem, and we'll understand that you were right the whole time."

So what happened? He took the field, had no problems, and started to feel okay again (or continued to feel okay?).

All of the pieces were beginning to fit into place, and I was increasingly confident we were going to Athens this year. In other words: *zeru tituli*, my ass.

CHAPTER 25

The Perfect Match,
Played the Night Before

In the winter of 2007, Greece was already in our sights. The important thing was to know how to wait, and while we were biding our time, Milan bought Ronaldo from Real Madrid during the January transfer market. We were suspended midway between mythology and the history of art. The Phenomenon is a remarkable young man—an open, generous, sensitive, humble, shy person. He's the opposite of what everyone thinks of him. The only thing is, there was nothing driving him to train and exercise to attain the maximum he could achieve. And that really pissed me off. I had never had a striker of his quality; Ronie was, and remains, unrivaled in his field—the invention of a superior mind.

When he got to Milanello, he was a little overweight and, as a result—at least in the early period—he worked very hard. He wanted to lose weight, even though we already had some problems persuading him to work with a certain degree of continuity. He was remarkably gifted—unlike anyone else—and he thought that was enough to turn him into the Ronaldo of the old days. He was as wrong as he could be. We needed him for the championship season. I used to tell him that, and he would listen to me, but not that carefully. We considered his arrival to be a huge gamble; at first, he believed in it along with us, when we were all still rowing in the same direction. Then he seemed to give up; just as he started scoring goals, he got lazy, and, from that point forward, we all lost our bets. Him first, followed by A. C. Milan.

Ronie just rested on his laurels. It was a real pity, because he still had enormous potential. I was positive that he could become the greatest footballer on earth; he had everything he needed to do it, except for one thing: the sheer will. At first, we got along like a house on fire, but once he started to show his indifference I got tired of pushing him. There was no point in getting angry, so I thought: "Okay, we'll work on it next summer." It proved impossible: an injury intervened. First one, then another, and then another still, until he had the operation in Paris. If he'd only worked just a little harder . . .

And I have to say that, in the locker room, everybody was happy to see him. I've heard people say that at A. C. Milan we take surveys of the more experienced veteran players before completing the acquisition of a major player. That's not exactly accurate, but it's not that far from the real situation, either. When a player of a certain importance is about to join the team, we listen to the impressions of his future teammates, but we don't ask for their opinions. The players don't have a veto, but they can voice their concerns. For example, Christian Poulsen, long before joining Juventus, had a physical examination with us. He wasn't too popular in the locker room, but that's not why we decided not to take him in the end. He had a problem with his ankle, and the doctors said no. It was a different matter with Antonio Cassano: he would not have been likely to fit in with our group.

Together with Ronaldo, that January transfer window brought us Massimo Oddo from Lazio, the right fullback who could make Cafu huff and puff—another brick in the road that was leading to the final game in Athens. By now it was an obsession; I thought about it all the time, with one eye on Liverpool and the other on A. C. Milan—half my mind on the Italian championship and the other on the Champions League. In the first round, we struggled against Celtic. In the quarterfinals, we played Bayern Munich; we finished 2–2 at home, to the great concern and frenzy of one and all, while Galliani was busy unscrewing the last bolt holding my bench in place. He had almost finished the job. In fact, when we played the away game at the Allianz Arena, Milan had two coaches: me and the ghost of Marcello Lippi, who had already come to an agreement to replace me. If we had been eliminated from the European Cup, Berlusconi would certainly have eliminated me.

During that whole period, the players were great—caring and kind. They let me know they were rooting for me. They weren't indifferent to what was happening. In Munich, thanks to Ambrosini, I rediscovered the beloved Christmas Tree formation. We won 2–0. Even Pippo scored: he aimed at the bottom right corner, the ball wound up in the top left corner, from an offside position. It was a classic Inzaghi-style goal. We went to the semifinals against Manchester United, with Liverpool against Chelsea; come on, we can do this.

The first match was at Old Trafford. We were ahead, 2–1; we lost 3–2. I turned into a genuine oaf. Sir Alex Ferguson invited me, according to tradition, to have a glass of wine with him in his office, but I didn't go; I was too angry. "Get drunk by yourself, Ancelotti, that's a better idea." Before the second leg, I took him a bottle of Tignanello as an apology. It's a Tuscan red, maybe sixty euros a bottle, something like that—not three hundred euros a bottle, the way they do at Inter.

The second leg of the semifinal was a perfect match. We played as if we were in an enchanted world. We felt like Alice in Wonderland, but we were the wonders. Ninety minutes of excitement and glory. Thrills and shivers from the cold, because it was raining like God really meant it, which made it all the more magical. The classic question I get from the fans is, Where did you get that monstrous level of performance—that incredible 3–0 game, with goals by Kaká, Seedorf, and Gilardino? Fifty percent in Istanbul and fifty percent in Milanello the evening before.

Twenty-four hours before we played, Liverpool had played its home semifinal game against Chelsea. That evening, our athletic center, for all practical purposes, no longer existed; it had been replaced by a bank of stands. The mythical Kop of Anfield had been moved to Carnago, in the province of Varese, the hearth and threshold of the *rossineri* world. The party was here in our meeting rooms, with thirty bloodthirsty fans hunkered around the television set.

You'll Never Walk Alone, Liverpool. There we were, *Milanisti* wrapped in red scarves. We were shouting and howling against Chelsea (I solemnly swear it'll never happen again . . .); Liverpool team hats and toy trumpets were pulled out at one point. It was one chorus after another. The only things missing were bottles of beer and free-form belching, otherwise the ceremony was complete. It went just as we had hoped. Liverpool made it to the finals. Whereupon we all looked one another in the face and thought the same thing: We've already won. Against Manchester and against Liverpool. We could even have skipped the matches, it was all written by destiny. Milan fans know the second perfect game very well—the one against Liverpool. What they don't know is that, in fact, we had already played it the day before.

Athens, here we come. I told you that's how it would turn out, boys. Galliani in the meantime was exhausted, his arm was sore; he'd had to retighten all the bolts on my bench. There was a sense of euphoria that is still impossible to describe. We knew that the Champions League was ours for the taking, while Liverpool knew they were doomed. Until just a few hours before the final match, I nurtured only a single doubt, concerning the striker. I hadn't decided who would play that position, Gilardino or Inzaghi. Alberto was feeling better, while Pippo was Pippo. Even though they'd never admit it now, a number of players came to ask me one thing: "You aren't thinking of letting Pippo play, are you? Don't you see the shape he's in?"

He was indeed half dead, and yet I knew that those were his nights. And before a challenge of that sort, everyone shows up, clamoring for a position, even guys on crutches. Ready to go out on the field, from the first minute to the last. I chose Inzaghi, and he gave us the European Cup with a double.

I don't actually remember that much about the game, but I remember everything about the aftermath. We were in our hotel, by the big and luxurious swimming pool, just outside of Athens. There was a party with a hundred or so people, and when the outsiders finally left, we went over to poolside, where there was a little bar for the hotel guests, a sort of kiosk. We drank it dry in the first five minutes; not a drop of alcohol was left untouched. Whiskey, Sambuca, rum, grappa, beer: it was all slurped down in one massive collective gulp. Those of us who weren't completely sloshed started a running bet on who would be the first to fall into the pool; we were all at high risk of drowning. We were stumbling, but we were determined to keep partying. Since we were the European champions, we maintained a certain demeanor: no one fell in the pool, but many of us collapsed on the poolside asphalt—which hurt more. In the meantime, Serginho had wrapped his arms around me and was practically in tears: "Carlo, you are my father."

I did some rapid mental calculations; it just wasn't possible. "What are you saying, Sergio? You're older than me ..."

"You're my dad."

"No, Sergio, really. You're far too ugly to be my son."

"Dad ..."

"Cut it out. How the hell can I explain this to Katia and Davide, my two real children?"

And he started tousling my hair, like a three-year-old. How the fuck had we ever won the championship? The cup—poor little thing—had wound up in bed with Galliani, once again. Maybe this was true love.

Before long, our managing director would have a second chance, when we won the European Super Cup (against Seville) and the International Cup (A. C. Milan–Boca Juniors, 4–2, and our chance at vindication—a way to forget the final we lost to them in 2003). Every cup we lift into the air means a night of torrid love for Galliani. That's why he hated it when we lost.

CHAPTER 26

Once Upon a Time,
I Signed a Contract with Real Madrid

Tortellini *y merengues*, the royal banquet is served. Look at it
and you'll gain weight; eat it and you'll go down in history.
The history of a city, a team, a nation. An actor in a stunningly
beautiful movie. *Camiseta blanca* and a dinner jacket. I was invited
to the royal ball, and I went: "Don Carlo, Señores. I am here to
train you."

In 2006, I accepted an offer from Real Madrid, and, I have to
say, it wasn't a difficult decision. A wonderful prospect, the scent
of life. It was April 2006, and A. C. Milan's triumphant return,
crowned in Athens, had not yet begun, but Real Madrid had already
understood everything: "We want you. You're the best." The Best,
because the title of The Special One had already been taken: José
Mourinho had assigned it, to none other than José Mourinho.

I was curious to understand what it was like to live on a normal team bench, without excessive tremors and vibrations under my ass. They came looking for me, and I signed happily. A preliminary contract, for three years, and fifteen million euros—five million euros a season, almost twice what I was earning at Milan. Pure, unadulterated luxury. Independent journalists had sensed that something was going on, and they reported on it; less independent journalists took care of denying everything on my behalf. Too kind, you really shouldn't have.

During negotiations, I never met Florentino Pérez in person, but undoubtedly he had been the first to suggest my name. He was the *jefe* of just about everything, the second king of Spain, after Juan Carlos. He wrote the shopping list. He had put down my name, and it was an exciting thing. The only problem was that they'd need a plus-size grocery cart to hold me. The idea of me at the Estadio Santiago Bernabéu; let's just hope nobody calls security.

The decisive meeting had been in Milan over dinner, between me and Ramón Martínez, who was Real Madrid's technical director at the time. We spent a couple of hours talking about players and the reason that I had been first choice: "We like the way you deploy your team, we like the way you think about football, you're the one we need for what we're trying to do. So please entertain us, *señor*." What with jokes and goals, I figured I could do that. There was just one obstacle to overcome, and it wasn't exactly a secondary problem: my contract with Milan. That good old wobbly bench of mine. "If they release me from my contract, then there's no problem, I'm all yours. One thing is for sure: I don't want to force anyone's hand, and, most importantly, I don't want to start a fight with my club—or at least what I consider my club until proven otherwise." Until that point, Milan knew nothing about our talks.

The other person I talked to at Real Madrid—or El Madrid, as they tend to call it—was José Ángel Sánchez, who was the de facto chief administrative officer of the club. He was in charge of contracts; he handled the dubloons and the major decisions. Everyone was in agreement: I was going to be the new coach.

"Ancelotti, in the next couple of hours, we're going to send you a fax at your office in Milanello."

"No, listen, it might be better if you sent it to my house."

Yes, that way we could avert a scene out of a horror film: a sheet of paper feeds out of the fax machine, and the walls of Milanello begin to crumble. Down tumbles the photograph of Berlusconi, followed by the pictures of me, and all the photographs of the triumphs of Milan, the *rossineri*. One wall collapses against the next and takes it down in turn, like dominoes falling. Summon an exorcist, put everyone into quarantine. In that dire setting, even the ghost that Capello claimed he heard every night would reveal himself, clanking his chains. No question, that was a scenario I'd rather avoid. And, in fact, they sent the pre-contract to my house in Felegara, where framed pictures and walls remained soundly in place, guarded by my watchdogs, one of whom is named Nelson. (Any reference to Dida is completely and fondly intentional.)

Six sheets of paper, total; simple, without Real Madrid letterhead. In it was everything they had promised me. Everything. I didn't ask for the moon, but I came close. And they kept their word. I never had any reason to doubt they would. They were reliable people. I understood that from the very beginning. I signed it and returned it to sender. I sat staring at the fax machine; as it swallowed the sheets of paper, it looked like a hungry child. I may even have emitted an excited "¡Olé!"

At the bottom of that pre-contract there was a rider. It was a clause on which I had insisted: "This contract will become valid only once A. C. Milan gives its consent." There was still one major step. At that point, I became an ambassador on my own behalf; I called Galliani, with a serious voice that was nothing like me, and I was concise and laconic: "Signore Galliani, I need to see you."

"Come when you like. My office at headquarters, in Via Turati."

There, Galliani is playing on home turf; he has all his familiar moves, he even knows where to seat people with whom he has to negotiate—or arm wrestle. When Gattuso was on the verge of leaving the team to go to Bayern Munich, for example, Galliani summoned him to Milan and locked him up in the trophy room. "Rino, look around you carefully, and then let's talk it over." He convinced him to stay by wearing him out.

That day, I started talking first, beating Galliani to the punch: "Listen, I asked for this meeting because I have a major opportunity. I've had an offer, apparently, from Real Madrid." I qualified it in an attempt at diplomacy. "It's an opportunity that I'd really like to take advantage of, because we're talking about one of the most important soccer clubs on earth. Here, I've won and won and won again. I've been here as a player and as a coach, I know everything and everyone; maybe it's a good time to seek greener pastures. I see it as a challenge, it could really teach me a lot, it would be exciting. If you could just see your way to ..."

I was starting to blabber on, and I also had a vaguely doleful expression on my face, as if to say: make new friends, but keep the old; one is silver but the other is gold. Oh, of course I'd get used to the new situation; finding my footing between one championship and the next was becoming my specialty. I'd made my decision. But so had Galliani. And his decision wasn't the same as mine: "That's entirely out of the question."

"Excuse me?"

"That's entirely out of the question, Carletto. You stay here, we'll extend your contract. We don't want to give you up. We need the work you do here. We must go forward together."

I'll confess that at times like that I felt like a genuine musketeer. One for all and all for one—which can be rendered in its Milan-fan slang version: Berlusconi for all, and all for Berlusconi.

Galliani went on: "You've done great work here with us, so I can't let you leave. At this point in time, there is no such thing as A. C. Milan without you. Our story hasn't come to an end yet."

"But..."

"No buts. You are, and you will remain, the coach of A. C. Milan."

It was as if he were symbolically handing me all the nuts and bolts he had removed from my bench over the years. Only symbolically, of course; otherwise, it would have taken a three-quarter-ton truck to haul off all that scrap metal. And I didn't happen to have one with me.

I have to say I took it well. Very well. "If that's how things stand, Signore Galliani, then I'll be delighted to stay on."

"I repeat, we'll extend your contract and adjust it to your satisfaction."

That wasn't really what mattered. The important thing was the faith he had expressed in me. No price can be set on feeling loved and valued. These are emotions, and therefore priceless. When Real Madrid told me, "You're the best," they had certainly hit the right note—the same note that the Triad had sounded a few years before them. Cuddle me and feed me, and I'm happy.

So I called up Real Madrid and told them about my conversation with Galliani: "He told me that I can't accept your offer. But I thank you; it's been an honor to negotiate with you." At home, I still have that pre-contract in a box with all my most important things. It's a souvenir of a nice, adrenaline-charged period. Ramón Martínez was very nice to me: "I expected it to turn out this way, but it was a good experience for us too. We'll see you again; let's stay in touch."

At that point, they focused their attention on Fabio Capello, who had already worked for them once. The Spanish press began pairing his name with mine in articles. The way they told it, it had turned into a battle between him and me, an all-Italian derby; in reality, I had already signed a pre-contract, but I had also already rejected their offer. At a certain point, Capello got angry and issued a statement that made me smile with fond indulgence: "You think Real Madrid wants Ancelotti? Excuse me, but whom did they call first?"

He thought he was the only candidate; actually—that time, at least—they had called me first, and I had even answered. Often my friends make jokes about that famous phrase. Whenever I invite one of them for dinner: "Sure, Carletto, we'll be there. But whom did you invite first?" It's become a catchphrase, an all-purpose joke.

People have called me from Real Madrid. There have been numerous contacts between Florentino Pérez and me; we've chatted and traded opinions. He is a person I respect; he knows what he's doing and what he wants. He loves Real Madrid first and foremost; he's a softhearted romantic, just like me. We like soccer, we love life, we enjoy entertaining people. We see eye-to-eye on many points. The last time we talked, he told me one thing in particular: "Carlo, someday you will be my coach."

CHAPTER 27

We'll Beat the Bastard

I never engaged in doping when I played soccer. I took adrenal-cortex injections, like everyone did, but it was legal and legitimate. You were allowed. Some doctors even prescribed it. "It helps to recover from fatigue," they told us, and, in fact, you felt less tired. Today, I am slightly dopey, but that state of mental confusion is a result of age—of my endless nomadic roaming, in my thoughts, from A. C. Milan to Real Madrid, from A. S. Roma to Chelsea and the national team of the Ivory Coast. That is why, whenever a soccer player suffering from ALS comes forward, I am so enormously irritated to hear people say that it's all because of the substances that were circulating in the locker rooms. What do they know about it? Why don't they find out the facts before they open their mouths? A bunch of self-appointed doctors without licenses. I get mad, just as Stefano Borgonovo gets mad. Stefano is the person who helped me decide to write this book. He is suffering from ALS, but "not caused by doping," as he often says. He fights against his personal enemy and the ignorance of the general public. There is a foundation that bears his name.

The reason I wrote this autobiography was to help Stefano. Anything I earn from its publication will be donated to research, because while fans may want to know everything about me, I want to know everything about this disease, and especially one thing in particular: the best way to beat the bastard, as Stefano calls his illness. He has lived in the shadows for two years, ashamed to show his face in public. Then he understood: life is beautiful, and we need to do our best to defend it. We need to fight for life, at Stefano's side.

In soccer circles, rumors had been circulating for years that something was wrong with Borgonovo. It was an insistent rumor, but no one knew anything for certain. He only emerged once he felt ready: "Friends, I'm not well, that's for sure. But there is one thing I want to say: the Bastard has already done me enough harm—no more." He contacted Galliani to organize an exhibition game in Florence between A. C. Milan and Fiorentina (the two teams he played for), he gave an interview to Sky TV, he put his name and reputation into it. He took an enormous risk. It wasn't easy for someone in his condition. He was clear-minded, but he exhibited the symptoms of his disease: "Here I am, ladies and gentlemen. I am Stefano Borgonovo. And I want to win."

That was the beginning of the Great Challenge on the soccer field, with Ruud Gullit's tears and my own sense of helplessness. I saw Stefano in a wheelchair and didn't know how to react; I didn't know what to say, how to treat him. I hadn't seen him for many years, and I never thought he'd look like this when I saw him again. We were all weeping, while he was laughing, and that's what helped us to sweep away the barriers and prejudices.

To think back on it now, we really did act like idiots; he needed our support, and we just pulled out our handkerchiefs and started sobbing. It was paradoxical that Stefano bolstered our courage, and not the other way around. His brain travels at a supersonic speed, he's faster than any of us, and, that evening at the Stadio Artemio Franchi, he'd already outdistanced us completely. We were thinking, it's not possible that he is sick, while he was thinking, it is possible to find a cure.

At that point, I was still shocked and, to tell the truth, somewhat uncomfortable. Once we got back to Milan, Mauro Tassotti and Filippo Galli both told me that they had talked with him: "Carletto, Stefano asked us to go see him." So I got over my reluctance and got into my car, and drove to his house, in Giussano. I was worried; I was afraid that I would freeze up in his presence, be unable to speak, go blank. Instead, the minute I entered his room I felt fine, I was at ease. Stefano talks through the voice of a computer. He speaks with his eyes, in the most literal sense. He moves his eyes to pick out letters on a display, forming words and phrases and sentences. All you need to do, though, is look at his eyes to understand a great many things, first and foremost that he is more alive than all the rest of us put together. When they say that the eyes are the windows to the soul, that's a simplification. For him, they are the keys to escape prison—two glittering beams of hope.

The first thing he said to me was, "Do you remember that time when we were on the National team?"

"No, Stefano."

He started writing an anecdote, word by word, laboriously. And as he wrote, I began to understand how that story was going to end. For me: badly.

"Carletto, you really can't remember what a fool you made of yourself that time?"

Okay, now I'm starting to remember. Unfortunately.

"We were in summer training at Trigoria; you, me, and Roberto Baggio all in the same room. It was hot out, the middle of the summer, and we were telling jokes and kidding around. At a certain point, you decided to exaggerate. You went too far. You opened the window and you took off your undershirt, with a draft right on your back. There was no air conditioning..."

"Okay, Stefano, that's enough. This is ancient history."

"No, no, let me tell the story. I told you it was damp out, that you could get sick, but you said not to worry, that you were *de fero*. That's right, with a Roman accent, *de fero*—an iron man. We were laughing and kidding around."

Some people might wonder what was so bad about what I did, and, in fact, I asked Stefano the same thing (alas!). "The next morning, you woke up with a fever of 104 and strep throat. Baggio and I came to see you to ask how the iron man was doing. You threw a shoe at us. And you left summer training camp because you were a wreck."

At that point, I really felt like an ass, for two reasons. First, that day at Trigoria I had proven that I was an ass. Second, I was an ass the first time I saw Stefano sick, because I thought that he was somehow different from me. In fact, I hadn't understood a thing. When he was a soccer player, he was lazy, he lacked intensity in his playing, but now he has become a warrior. A soldier who never surrenders. He wants to win every battle, by whatever means necessary, and he will succeed this time, too.

I had misgivings about Stefano, and he helped me to overcome them. Me and many others—all his friends. And then Kaká and David Beckham, whom I took to his house. Stefano wanted to meet them in person to explain the situation to them. He believes that everyone can do something for him: support research to find a solution for his problem, and help the families of those afflicted with the disease, because treating the disease is often prohibitively expensive. Stefano already had Beckham's autograph, on an England jersey that Capello had sent him. He had enormous respect for Kaká.

He tells everyone the same thing: "I know I can do this, but not alone. I need a team. The more of us there are, the better."

I'm in, I can coach. Stefano's the striker. The Bastard is the goalkeeper on the opposing team. We'll force in a goal. We'll win.

CHAPTER 28

Summoned by Abramovich.
The End.

Thank you. Quite simply, thank you. If I am Carletto Ancelotti, I owe it all to Italian football. I feel like an authentic product of my homeland, a genuine, official soccer player and coach. A 100-percent Italian product. For export, sooner or later, because the soul never changes: it goes well beyond the concept of borders. They raised me the way my father cultivated the soil; I grew because I was nourished with passion. In much the same way that he could predict the weather by looking at the sky, I could tell the future by interpreting DVDs—my present and my future. Whatever team I may be coaching, my last thought is for many people. Thanks again. *Grazie. Gracias. Thank you. Danke.* In all the languages of Europe.

GRAZIE: I played in Serie A and on the national team, I won, I trained, I coached, and I won again. I passed the ball to van Basten,

I tried to stop Maradona, I explained soccer to Del Piero, Maldini, Zidane, Kaká (and, in an attempt to win him over, the rich tycoons at Manchester City called me up in January 2009: that was their first time), Beckham, and Ronaldinho. I wept, I smiled, I lived just as I wanted to live, with excitement and passion. I always took home a salary without ever really noticing that I was working, like fat and happy pastry chefs. They eat to work, not the other way around, and that may be why I have a certain tendency to spread and grow. I have broad hips and a vast heart. I am head over heels in love with what I do. Thank you. Thanks again. For everything that Italian soccer has given me. Much more than what I was able to give in return, even though I have been pretty generous. I experienced and learned a single and unified culture, that of results before everything else. The soccer we play is intervillage rivalry taken to its logical extreme.

But that's all right. When I see kids playing in a little field, I get emotional. This is the point we're at: "Go, boys, only one out of a thousand ever makes it." Without wanting a lawsuit from Gianni Morandi for the lyrics of the song, I can safely state that I am that one out of a thousand.

April 1, 2009, was an interesting day. I don't think I'm an April fool; if anything, I'm good for the whole year. More than a fluke of destiny, let's say it was a bit of April foolishness. That fits with my personality. Until seven in the evening, I was mostly thinking in English. After lunch, I gave an interview to the Sky TV channel, which I still remember in considerable detail. That's what happens on special days, whether good or bad—they are in any case unforgettable.

"Carlo, what do you see in your future?"

"I have a contract until 2010 with A. C. Milan, so I'm staying."

"Can we say that you are staying for certain?"

"You can say that I'm staying."

"How many lies have you told in this interview?"

"One or two, a few, just to defend myself..."

"If we see you again in a couple of months, will we be able to say which of the things you just told us are lies?"

"In a couple of months, sure."

In other words, I was making it clear, in the gentlest way imaginable, that I would be leaving. Certainly I was starting to prepare for my departure, sowing the seeds for it. I had been taking intensive English lessons for a while, and it was no accident. Three lessons a week, a model student. *The pen is on the table, and my name is Carlo.* That afternoon, I answered the questions with a ferocious expression on my face I had learned how to adopt, because I knew what the next phase was likely to be. An appointment that evening in Adriano Galliani's office at number 3, Via Turati. Headquarters, once again. A scene I'd already seen and experienced. Déjà vu. The same characters but a brand new proposal (much more than a proposal...). In some ways, an indecent proposal. The proposal from Chelsea Football Club.

"Good evening, Carletto."

"Good evening, Mr. Galliani."

His expression was darker than mine, I started feeling shivers running up my back. Shivers of joy, among other things. It was a surprise.

"Listen, Galliani, I have something to tell you. I'm thinking of going to coach Chelsea."

"That's entirely out of the question."

Brusque. Verging on the violent. My vice president was like a broken record. It was the same answer he gave when he refused to let me leave to coach Real Madrid. The same six words—seven, if you include the contraction.

"So you want me to stay?"

"Of course we want you to stay."

Our meeting continued over dinner, at Da Giannino, the restaurant in Milan where people meet to negotiate contracts and deals. In reality, it was already all decided, but we did our best to work out an understanding: "We'll make the final decision after the end of the championship finals, so after May 31. In the meantime, we'll qualify for the next Champions League."

There were almost two months to go. We were in the big room, the one with the megascreen television. We watched Italy vs. Ireland, Giovanni Trapattoni against Marcello Lippi, whom some people already considered my designated successor from 2010 on, after the South Africa World Cup. I felt light on my feet, even though I looked like a bull, and that was the real miracle. A homemade miracle, just to be clear—not something crafted in the luxurious drawing room of His Mourinho-ness. He, while the game was being broadcast live, was on the Piero Chiambretti show, comparing Himself to Jesus. Forgive him, for he knows not what he says. I do. And I often think of everything that led up to this day.

My life has a specific and illogical explanation. It's based on the secret of dreams: you have them without believing in them too intensely, and that relieves the pressure. At least at first. There was a time when my idol was Gene Gnocchi, to give just one example. A number 10 shirt with a comic strip printed on it. He thought with his feet and played with his head. Then my role models changed, I grew, because my progress in Italy was step by step. Put all your effort into it, and you'll see that something will emerge. As a player, I won four Italian Cups, three Scudetti, an Italian Super Cup, two Champions Cups, two European Super Cups, and two Intercontinental Cups. As a coach, I won an Italian Cup, a Scudetto, an Italian Super Cup, two Champions Leagues, two European Super Cups, and a FIFA Club World Cup. That's a lot, but the numbers don't really convey the idea. Pride lies elsewhere, where emotion intervenes. You have to try it to believe. And feel it to live. A normal, wonderful narrative. Between a field and a wobbly bench, I spent my best years at A. C. Milan. So, once again, thank you. Thank you to all those, from Reggiolo to heaven, whom I met along the way: friends, enemies, teammates, coaches, players. To the teams I coached and those I might still coach. In particular, thank you to Silvio Berlusconi for letting me discover a new world and for never telling me what formation to field. And to Galliani, with just this one regret: why didn't we ever use the informal "*tu*," why weren't we on a first-name basis? "I love you, Signore Galliani" is one thing, but "I love you Adriano, man" is much better.

THANK YOU: to the clubs that thought of me all the way from England. To Chelsea, of course, which was the first in chronological order. I will confess that, beginning at a certain point in the 2008–09 season, I watched a lot of DVDs of John Terry, Frank Lampard, and Didier Drogba. I was already the manager of the Blues, at least on paper. Just like with Real Madrid, a few seasons ago. Me and Abramovich together: things could be worse. Worse, which is something he can imagine—or actually remember, since he has already worked with His Specialness, José Mourinho...

GRACIAS: also to Florentino Pérez. As with Abramovich, whose first name is Roman, there's a bit of Italy in his given name. Florentino. And so it is natural that he possesses the inner art. A conversation with him always has the fine flavor of ancient things. Simple things. Real Madrid fills his soul, occupies his mind, which is candid—in a word, *blanca*. He has always greeted me with the same phrase, which I have already mentioned: "Carlo, someday you will be my coach." In the meantime, he now has his own original sin: he has only just begun to work with His Specialness.

DANKE: to Bayern Munich.

...the list could go on, and it could include certain other people. It's not hard to imagine who or why. And, as I express my thanks, I raise my eyes, I go back in time, and I remember. When I was coaching in Italy, I often looked at a fire alarm at Milanello. They installed it directly over my room, Room Number 5. On it, there is a phrase in white letters on a red background, and in case of emergency it lights up: LEAVE THE BUILDING IMMEDIATELY. On certain days it was turned off out of respect and, when things were tight, out of necessity. Then Abramovich and Chelsea Football Club arrived. The Premier League and the FA Cup. Now I want the Champions League. And I'll make a promise: if we win, there'll be a party. And Zhirkov won't sing.

Carlo Ancelotti

Born 1959 in Reggiolo, Reggio-Emilia

AS A PLAYER:

Parma A. C., 1974–1979
  Promoted to Serie A in 1979

A. S. Roma, 1979–1987
  Scudetto 1983
  Coppa Italia 1980, 1981, 1984, 1986
  European Cup runners-up 1984

A. C. Milan, 1987–1992
  Scudetto 1988, 1992
  Italian Supercup 1988
  European Cup 1989, 1990
  UEFA Super Cup 1989, 1990
  Intercontinental Cup 1989, 1990

Italian National Team, 1981–1991
  26 appearances
  World Cup squads 1986, 1990

AS A MANAGER:

Italian National Team, 1994
Assistant coach to Arrigo Sacchi
Runners-up, World Cup 1994

A. C. Reggiana, 1995–1996
Won promotion to Serie A, 1996

Parma, 1996–1998
Runners-up in Serie A, 1997

Juventus, 1999–2001
Runners-up in Serie A 2000, 2001
Intertoto Cup 1999

A. C. Milan, 2001–2009
Scudetto 2004
Coppa Italia 2004
Supercoppa Italiana 2004
European Cup 2003, 2007
UEFA Super Cup 2003, 2007
FIFA Club World Cup 2007

Chelsea F. C., 2009–present
Premier League 2010
F. A. Cup 2010
Community Shield 2009